ADVANCED ENGLISH SERIES

Troublesome Grammar

by Dr. Nan DeVincent-Hayes

Design by Kifer Graphics

Dedication:
I owe my family
my eternal gratitude
for understanding my work
and helping me to achieve it.

A very special thanks to **Elizabeth Sacca** of Ocean City, Maryland, for not only being a special friend and colleague but a wonderful critiquer of my work as well.

About the Author

Dr. Nan DeVincent-Hayes has ten published books to her credit and over 100 short stories and articles in such publications as *Redbook, Parade, Us, Brides, People,* and a host of others. A graduate of Villa Maria College of Gannon University, Dr. Hayes earned both her masters from Duquesene University, and her Ph.D, *Summa cum laude,* from the University of Maryland, College Park. She also attended writing programs at the University of Pittsburgh, the University of Rochester, and Middlebury College's Bread Loaf. She has served as Chair of the college's English department, as well as associate professor, and has taught for various universities.

Publis hed by:
Garlic Press
605 Powers St.
Eugene, OR 97402

ISBN 0-931993-19-9
Order Number GP-019

www.garlicpress.com

Table of Contents

Introduction

Having taught grammar on the elementary through college levels, it struck me that there are certain common problems that we all seem to grapple with. This book looks at those areas. The ins and outs of the English language can frustrate not only newcomers to our country, but those who are American-born, as well, and have spoken English since childhood. And with advancements in the scientific and technical fields, new terminology constantly is being created while some of the old vocabulary fall prey to archaism. Thus, keeping current of such changes is vital in the process of mastering English.

Because of the complexities and rigidity of our grammatical principles, some troublesome areas seem to plague us forever. Just when we think we have grasped all those grammar rules taught by our elementary school teachers, along comes something new and more perplexing, or something traditional with a new twist and all the more bewildering.

This book discusses some of the most common irksome grammatical points, and how they can be managed for better communication in writing and speaking. In this text, you'll find the old "bug-a-boos" presented in a different light so they can be more readily understood and put to use. Each chapter offers a simple pattern where one, or two or more major vexing topics are looked at through the use of an Introduction a General Rule for the subject matter, and then examples and explanations. Thus a blue print for how this book is laid out consists of:

I. Introduction (to the entire chapter)
II. General Rule (overview of the principles of the points being taught
    Sections
    Players (examples of words pertaining to the section)
    Model (right and wrong illustrations of the principle being taught)
    Rule Application (how the criteria pertain to the model)
    Model Explanation (concise instruction on how to fix the 'wrong example" and what is correct about the "right" example)
III. Summary (review of the entire chapter)
IV. Drill (exercises in the lesson being taught)

The book also contains a Cumulative Exam and answer keys for the exam and all the drills.

Such a nonthreatening learning pattern as presented here is easy to comprehend, fun to work with, effective to review, and simple to cross-reference with the content's other subject matter.

So when those sticky grammar hang-ups confront you, or you just want a concise review or a refresher course, or you'd like to have supplemental material for what is being taught in the classroom, turn the pages here and you'll find all the help you need in a hassle-free manner.

Enjoy,

Dr. Nan DeVincentis-Hayes

Dr. Nan DeVincentis Hayes
Author

Agreement
SUBJECTS, VERBS, AND PRONOUNS

In writing, it's important that words in sentences agree with one another so that readers can infer your intended meaning. Agreement particularly applies to subjects, verbs, and nouns. For example, it would be erroneous to write:

> The students *throws* a football during *his* recess.

Since the subject, *students*, is plural, the verb must also be plural. The word *throw* indicates plurality while *throws* is used for a single subject (student). Likewise, to use the pronoun *his* is incorrect because this pronoun refers to a single student. The correct pronoun in this sentence would be *their*.

> The students *throw* a football during *their* recess.

SECTION 1:

Plural Subjects

PLAYERS:

Verbs—show action
Subjects—the things/persons being acted on
Pronouns—antecedent references (he, she, it, they, their, them)

Plural subjects (more than one) require plural verbs and plural pronouns. Below are examples:

MODEL

                                     S   V   Prn   N

Wrong: The **firemen aims his hose** at the burning building.

                                       S   V   Prn   N

Right: The **firemen aim their hoses** at the burning building.

Model Explanation:

The subject, *firemen*, is plural; therefore, the predicate or verb, *aims*, must be pluralized to *aim*, so that there is agreement. Likewise, since the subject

---

GENERAL RULE:

To make subjects, verbs and pronouns agree, check that the verb tense and the number are the same, as well as the pronoun, if present. Personal pronouns must agree with their antecedents in number, gender, and person. Collective nouns are treated differently, as are nouns that always remain plural, nouns that change form to indicate number, nouns that are indefinite, and subjects that are combined by conjunctions. When in doubt, refer to a grammar or style book.

Rule application:

All parts of a sentence must agree with one another. Make subjects and predicates (verbs) agree with each other, and with any pronouns in the sentence.

refers to more than one firefighter, its pronoun reference, *his*, must also reflect more than one fireman, which in this case would require changing *his* (singular) to *their* (plural). It would also seem that since many firefighters are hosing the building, there must be more than one hose, and, thus, the sentence should reflect this by changing the singular *hose* to the plural *hoses*.

SECTION 2:

Compound Subjects

As is true with words in a sentence that reflect plurality (as seen above), compound subjects also require plural predicates or verbs, and pronouns.

Rule application:

All words in a sentence must agree with one another. Compound subjects, as is true with plural subjects, require plural predicates.

MODEL

```
                    ------------CS------------    V      P
Wrong:    Bob and Mary feeds its cat three times a day.

                    ------------CS------------    V      P
Right:    Bob and Mary feed their cat three times a day.
```

Model Explanation:

The compound subject, *Bob and Mary*, indicates two people, and thus is plural. Since *feeds* is singular, the plural *feed* is necessary. The pronoun *its* doesn't refer to *Bob and Mary* who are people, but rather reflects a "thing." Since *Bob and Mary* is a plural, a plural subject pronoun is needed, and the word *their* best suits this sentence.

SECTION 3:

Singular subjects following predicate

The subject of a sentence is sometimes difficult to determine when the sentence structure is confusing.

Here's an example.

Rule application:

Singular subjects require singular verbs, and singular verbs take singular subjects.

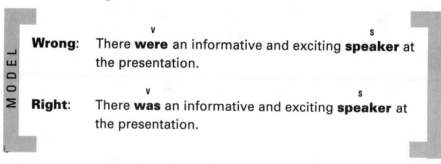

```
                              V                                    S
Wrong:    There were an informative and exciting speaker at
          the presentation.

                              V                                    S
Right:    There was an informative and exciting speaker at
          the presentation.
```

Model Explanation:

The word *there* throws readers off when it comes to determining the subject. Although it appears that *there* should be the subject, it isn't. *Speaker* is singular (only one speaker), so it requires a singular predicate. *Were* is a plural verb from the form *to be*, so it's not in agreement with the singular subject. *Was* is the singular form that should be used with *speaker*.

SECTION 4:

Double Plural Subjects

Any subject—whether compound in nature or plural in word—requires a predicate of agreement. Consider this example.

MODEL

>   s   s   v
> **Wrong:** The **children** and band **leaders sings** well for **its** school.
>
>   s   s   v
> **Right:** The **children** and band **leaders sing** well for **their** school.

Rule Application:

Plural subjects must have plural verbs and pronouns; this is true for subjects that are compound in nature, or plural in form.

Model Explanation:

The subject *children* is plural in nature without even considering that the word *leaders* is also plural. Thus, plural subjects require plural verbs. In the **wrong** example the predicate *sings* is singular in nature and, hence, the wrong verb. *Sing* is what is needed. Likewise, plural subjects command plural pronouns. *Its* is wrong in number and in gender; *their* is correct in gender (meaning people, not things), and correct in number (more than one in the subject).

SECTION 5:

Singular Subject in Prepositional Phrase

While singular subjects of sentences require singular predicates, singular subjects in prepositional phrases also require singular predicates.

MODEL

>   s   ----------PP---------- ---------- V----------
> **Wrong:** A **group** of preachers **are giving** a Bible class in the church hall.
>
>   s   ----------PP---------- --------V--------
> **Right:** A **group** of preachers **is giving** a Bible class in the church hall.

Rule Application:

Singular subjects in prepositional phrases take singular verbs.

Model Explanation:

The word *group* is the subject (S) in the prepositional phrase (PP) *of a group of preachers*. Since it is singular, its verb or predicate must also be singular. Hence, *are giving* is plural in nature; not singular. Thus, its use here is wrong.

Subjects Joined by "and"

The use of conjunctions changes the agreement of a sentence as seen here:

Rule Application:

When subjects are joined by a conjunction (such as the word *and*), they are considered to be compound plurals, and thus must take a plural verb or predicate.

MODEL

Wrong: Does the **team and the coach travel** in the same bus to "away games"?

Right: Do the **team and the coach travel** in the same bus to "away games"?

Model Explanation:

The above model has two subjects: *team* and *coach*, both of which are joined by the conjunction *and*. Therefore, the verb predicate must also be plural. *Does travel* is singular, so it doesn't agree with the plural subject, but *do travel* does agree. Notice that though the predicate is separated by other words in this example, the verb and subject must still agree.

Subjects Joined by "neither-nor"

"Neither/nor" affects the agreement of a sentence.

Rule Application:

When subjects are connected by *neither/nor,* the verb (predicate) should agree with the subject closest to it.

MODEL

Wrong: Neither the **teacher nor** the **students is telling** the principal about the mouse in the cafeteria.

Right: Neither the **teacher nor** the **students are telling** the principal about the mouse in the cafeteria.

Model Explanation:

Although the word *nor* is a conjunction, *neither* may act as an adjective, indefinite pronoun, or a conjunction. In the above example, two subjects—*teacher* and *students*—affect the predicate. The word *teacher* is singular and should take a singular verb but *students* is a plural subject and should take a plural predicate. Since *nor* precedes *students*, the verb should agree with the subject closest to it. Here, *students* is plural, making the predicate (*are telling*) plural. If the words *students* had been singular (*student*), then the verb *is telling* would have been correct.

SECTION 8:

Indefinite Pronoun Subjects

"Indefinite" pronouns make no reference to a particular person; thus, they affect the predicate.

Players:

Examples of indefinite pronouns (IP) include but aren't limited to:

someone	somebody	each
everyone	anyone	each one
anything	another	anybody
everything	no one	either
everybody	nobody	neither
many	few	several
both	all	none
some	more	most
any	either one	one

MODEL

                     S   IP   V

Wrong: **Anyone** who **want** to attend college should be able to afford it through government assistance.

                     S   IP   V

Right: **Anyone** who **wants** to attend college should be able to afford it through government assistance.

Rule Application:

IPs are considered singular in number, and thus command singular predicates.

Model Explanation:

Even though indefinite pronouns may seem as though they should be plural in nature, they are singular and take a singular verb. In the above example, **anyone** is an indefinite pronoun acting as the sentence's subject. In that capacity, its predicate must also be singular in order to be in agreement with the subject.

SECTION 9:

Plural or Singular Subjects (Collective Nouns)

Some words have the ability to serve as singular or plural subjects. They are referred to as "collective" nouns.

Players:

Here is a list of some of the most common collective nouns.

school	populace	herd	community
union	group	team	parish
bevy	public	audience	bunch

citizenry	club	board	congregation
faculty	company	council	orchestra
league	family	nation	department
panel	band	news	gaggle
batch	corps	jury	clergy
chassis	class	pack	committee

Rule Application:

Some collective nouns act in both the singular and plural modes, depending on how they're used in context; mainly, though, they behave as singular subjects and thus require singular predicates. Collective nouns are plural when members of the group appear to act independently; they are singular when the group acts as one unit.

MODEL

                              S   V   P
Wrong: The **jury are** on **its** way out of the courtroom.

                              S   V   P
Right: The **jury is** on **its** way out of the courtroom.

Model Explanation:

In the above sentence, **jury** is understood to be singular because: 1) its members are acting as one unit and not as individuals going their own way; 2) the subject's pronoun reference is singular (*its*); thus the subject requires a singular predicate, which would be *is* instead of *are*.

SECTION 10:

Plural or Singular Nouns

Some words must change their form in order to connote plurality or singularity. These changes indicate whether a singular or plural predicate is needed.

Players

Here is a brief list of words that change form to indicate number.

SINGULAR	PLURAL
criterion	criteria
ox	oxen
focus	foci
alga	algae
hoof	hoofs (hooves)
appendix	appendices
goose	geese
tooth	teeth
thesis	theses
datum	data

Rule Application:

Subjects that change their form to make a word plural or singular must also have corresponding verbs for agreement.

MODEL

                     s   v

Wrong: All the **criterion** for this experiment **call** for 100%

                                   s   -------

accuracy in results; the **appendices will**

       -------v-----------

discusses those results in detail.

                     s   v

Right: All the **criteria** for this experiment **call** for 100%

                                  s   ----------- v------------

accuracy in results; the **appendices will discuss** those results in detail.

Model Explanation:

In the **wrong** example, the word *criterion* is singular but the verb *call* is plural. Thus, there is no agreement here between subject and predicate. Since the subject is definitely referring to more than one *criterion* as noted by the word "All" at the beginning of the sentence, we know the word *criteria* is correct, so the predicate has to be plural as well. Hence, *call* is plural and should remain as the predicate. The second part of the sentence uses a plural subject, *appendices* (notice that some grammarians accept the word "appendixes" as the plural of appendix); thus, a plural verb is needed in order to have agreement. *Discusses* is singular and should be changed to *discuss* to indicate plurality.

SECTION 11:

Nouns That Look Plural

Some nouns remain as plurals even though their role is singular.

Players:

This chart lists a few of the main nouns that always look plural but may be used in the singular number.

trousers	headquarters	mathematics	ethics
politics	cattle	pants	scissors
congratulations	themselves	clothes	physics
news	corps	earnings	

MODEL

                     s   v

Wrong: The **news cover** all angles and events.

                     s   v

Right: The **news covers** all angles and events.

Rule Application:

Nouns appearing plural in nature (with an "s" on the end) but are singular require singular verbs.

Model Explanation:

Some words may look plural but are truly singular, such as **news**; these words require singular verbs or predicates. In the **wrong** example, the predicate **cover** is plural, and thus makes the sentence incorrect. *Covers* is singular and should be the verb used.

As is the case for nouns that look plural but are singular (preceding chart), there are also nouns that look singular but also may be plural. These include: *fun, deer, dust,* among others. Their predicate number is determined by how they're used in context. Always refer to a dictionary when in doubt.

Summary

Nouns (subjects) must always be in agreement, in number, gender, and person, with their verbs (predicate) and pronoun reference. If a subject is singular in a sentence, its predicate and pronoun also must be singular. If the verb is plural, the subject and pronoun of that verb must be plural as well.

Certain types of nouns require special attention in some sentences. These consist of 1) nouns that look plural in nature; 2) nouns that may be plural or singular; 3) nouns that are collective; and 4) nouns that are joined by conjunctions. In nearly all these instances, the determination of person, number, and gender is based on how the nouns and/or verbs are used in the sentence. Most indefinite pronouns are singular in number.

Always refer to a style book or dictionary as a final authority on the matter.

Choose the correct verb to the corresponding subject.

Example:

Physics (<u>is</u>, are) fun and exciting.

Drill 1:

1. Everyone (is, are) here to help, but no one (is, are) moving too quickly.

2. "And here (is, are) Regis and Kathy Lee."

3. Either the President or the First Lady (is, are) taking the American public on a television White House tour.

4. Corey or Casey (is, are) conducting auditions.

5. Moviegoers wanting to see the much-hyped film (stand, stands) in the ticket line for long periods.

Choose the subject that agrees with the verb.

Example:

There are cookie (crumb, <u>crumbs</u>) on the kitchen table.

Drill 2:

1. The (medication, medications) the doctor prescribed is for high blood pressure.

2. The school panel (member, members) are deciding whether to redistrict the area.

3. Either my (cousin, cousins) or my (aunt, aunts) is arriving on the three o'clock flight.

4. It's either the (fork, forks) or the (spoon, spoons) that isn't set properly at the table.

5. (Chelsea and Allison, Chelsea or Allison) hasn't opted to try out for cheerleading.

6. Neither the (dogs, dog) nor the (cats, cat) is interested in the two toy (mouses, mice).

7. I have a (tooth, teeth) ache; or should I say, "My (teeth, tooth) aches"?

8. Those are the best song and dance (team, teams) I've ever seen.

Drill 3

Make the following sentence parts agree in person, gender, and number.

Example:
Neither Mark nor Kim (was, were) present at the hearing.

1. Somebody (has, have) forgotten (his, her, their) purse and gloves.

2. Everyone (has, have) his or her task done, so the directors, along with their secretaries, (is, are) going to evaluate how each job (was, were) done.

3. There (is, are) two excuses for the (new, news) being bad; one (is, are) that the (media, medium) never prints the facts right, while the other (excuse, excuses) is that bad (new, news) (get, gets) more attention than good news (do, does).

4. The earnings of blue collar workers (has, have) remained stable even though (workers, worker) have put in more hours per day over the last decade; therefore, this type of worker should try to improve (himself, themselves) by becoming better educated to move up through the (rank, ranks).

5. The group of enthusiastic and noisy youngsters (was, were) frightening the passersby, so the theater manager made all the group members (leave, leaves).

Regular and Irregular Verbs

Verbs may be finite (regular) or nonfinite (irregular) in nature. Nonfinite verbs may take the form of verbals (as in the past participle), which are types of verbs that lack subjects and tense, and behave more like nouns (nominals) or modifiers than finite verbs. This chapter looks at both finite and irregular verbs in their three principle forms: Infinitive (present) tense, past tense, and past participle.

Regular or finite verbs add *"ed"* and *"d"* to their form to indicate time in the past (<u>walk</u> + "ed" = *walk<u>ed</u>*). There are about a hundred finite verbs that form their past by not adding the "d" or "ed." Finite or regular verbs are noted by their number (singular or plural) and by person (first, second, third).

Irregular verbs have the <u>simple</u> form as their root or base form, often referring to the infinitive root of "to," as in *"to walk," "to sing."* Several of these forms maintain their simple form throughout, as in **cut, cut, cut**. Irregular verbs don't follow the pattern of adding *"d"* or *"ed"* to the ending of the infinitive form. Instead, they form their past tense and past participle in uncommon ways, such as **sing, sang, sung**. To determine an irregular verb's form, refer to a dictionary. There are over 200 irregular verbs, and few have any type of pattern for determining the form their past tense or past participle will take.

The <u>past</u> tense of both regular and irregular verbs implies something that has recently passed, while the <u>past participle</u> indicates that something has passed awhile ago. Putting verbs in their proper tenses in a progressive manner is referred to as "conjugation."

SECTION 1:

Regular Verbs

These verbs' past tense and past participles are created by adding the suffixes "d" or "ed."

Players:

Below are a few examples of how the past tense and past participles are formed.

PRESENT TENSE	PAST TENSE	PAST PARTICIPLE
clean	cleaned	cleaned
type	typed	typed
sympathize	sympathized	sympathized
wash	washed	washed
agree	agreed	agreed
plan	planned	planned
use	used	used

MODEL

Wrong: Dominic <u>hoped</u> to the store yesterday.

Right: Dominic <u>hopped</u> to the store yesterday.

Rule Application:

Some verbs require the doubling of the ending consonant in order to create the past forms.

Model Explanation:

In the above **wrong** example, the suffix's consonant is not doubled, and thus the verb comes across as a different word, *"hoped,"* instead of "hop**p**ed." The correct statement demonstrates how to double the consonant.

MODEL

Wrong: Darrin <u>had live</u> in Milwaukee for the last ten years.

Right: Darrin <u>had lived</u> in Milwaukee for the last ten years.

Rule Application:

When using auxiliary verbs (had, have, etc.) with regular verbs, place the ending consonant "d" or "ed" after the auxiliary verb and root verb.

Model Explanation:

In the above **right** example, the "helping" or "auxiliary" verb <u>"had,"</u> is used in conjunction with the regular verb <u>*"lived"*</u> to show past tense. The **wrong** example neglects the suffix *"d"* and thus the predicate or verb phrase isn't properly formed. Make certain the verb is correct in both auxiliary and root forms.

SECTION 2:

IRREGULAR VERBS

These verbs don't form their past tenses by adding "d" or "ed."

Players:

The following chart features a few examples of irregular verbs.

INFINITIVE/PRESENT TENSE	PAST TENSE	PAST PARTICIPLE
lie	lay	lain
lay	laid	laid
begin	began	begun
bite	bit	bitten
be	was, were	been
come	came	come
blow	blew	blown
draw	drew	drawn
lead	led	led
rise	rose	risen
write	wrote	written
let	let	let
hang (suspend)	hung	hung
hang (execute)	hanged	hanged
see	saw	seen
lend	lent	lent
give	gave	given
throw	threw	thrown
choose	chose	chosen
fall	fell	fallen
beat	beat	beaten

Players:

Verbs in the past participle form usually take auxiliary verbs.

EXAMPLES OF AUXILIARY VERBS USED WITH PAST PARTICIPLES			
have	would	may	was
has	should	might	be
will	could	can	been

Rule Application:

Since irregular verbs take their own form in the past tense, it's best to refer to a dictionary for their proper patterns for the past tense and past participle predicates.

MODEL

Wrong: The Beagle puppy <u>awoked</u> before her mother did.

Right: The Beagle puppy <u>had awakened</u> before her mother did.

Model Explanation:

The word "_awoked_" is not proper grammar. Since the sentence indicates that the action happened in the past, an auxiliary verb (as seen in the word "had") is needed for the past participle form. Past participles generally require helping or auxiliary verbs.

M O D E L

Wrong:	Chris's parents <u>hanged</u> Chris's mobile from the kitchen ceiling.
Right:	Chris's parents <u>hung</u> Chris's mobile from the kitchen ceiling.

Rule Application:

Use a dictionary to make certain the irregular verb is used in its proper form.

Model Explanation:

In the **wrong** statement, the word *hanged* is improper because it refers to a type of execution (hanging); in the **right** example, the word *hung* is correct because this verbal implies that something is being "suspended" in the air.

M O D E L

Wrong:	Ms. Freedom, our math teacher, <u>gone</u> over the algebra problems.
Right:	Ms. Freedom, our math teacher, <u>had gone</u> over the algebra problems.
	or
	Ms. Freedom, our math teacher, <u>went</u> over the algebra problems.

Rule Application:

Past participles or irregular verbs generally require helping verbs.

Model Explanation:

The verb *gone* is the past participle of its infinitive *"to go"* ("go, went, gone"), which, in this example, demonstrates that in the past, the teacher had reviewed the problems. The verb "gone" is a past participle that requires an **auxiliary** or **helping** modal or verb, as in the first correct statement: *had gone*. Since the sentence gives no indication how long ago the action occurred, the use of the past tense word, *went*, would also be proper.

M O D E L

Wrong:	The scar on Ebony's knee is from having <u>hurted</u> herself on the swings.
Right:	The scar on Ebony's knee is from having <u>hurt</u> herself on the swings.
	or
	The scar on Ebony's knee is from when she <u>had hurt</u> herself on the swing.

Rule application:

Irregular verbs don't add an "ed" or "d" to their suffixes. Instead, they may change form or require auxiliary verbs in their past participle mode.

Model Explanation:

The verb *hurt* is an irregular verb and thus takes on a unique pattern in its three parts. In this case, in its three forms (infinitive, past, past participle), <u>hurt</u> remains in the infinitive form: "hurt → hurt → hurt." The second correct version indicates that Ebony injured herself in the distant past. This is proper as well, since the statement gives no indication of how long ago the event happened.

SECTION 3:

Either/Or Verbs

Here, verbs that can be either irregular or regular are presented.

Players:

The following are examples of verbs that may present themselves either way.

VERBS APPEARING IN THE REGULAR (FINITE) OR IRREGULAR (NONFINITE) MODES

spring	sprang/sprung	sprung
light	lighted/lit	lighted/lit
sew	sewed	sewed/sewn
dive	dove/dived	dived
show	showed	showed/shown
prove	proved	proved/proven
stink	stank/stunk	stunk
burn	burned/burnt	burned/burnt
thrive	throve/thrived	thrived/thriven
wake	woke	waked (woken–British)
leap	leaped/leapt	leaped/leapt
sweat	sweat/sweated	sweated

Rule Application:

Verbs that can be either regular or irregular in form should be done so in proper context.

MODEL

Right: The lifeguard <u>dived</u> into the ocean to save the boy.

Also Correct: The lifeguard <u>dove</u> into the ocean to save the boy.

Model Explanation:

In the above two correct sentences, the verb form "*dive*" can be used as "*dived*" or "*dove*" in the past tense or past participle tense; the latter would require an auxiliary verb with it.   This verb is one of the few that works as a regular or irregular predicate.

Summary

Regular or finite verbs form their past tenses simply by the addition of "d" or "ed" to their ending consonants, which may require doubling of the last consonant, as in "hop → hop*p*ed." Irregular or nonfinite verbs (also referred to as verbals) follow no specific rules about how to form their past tenses, and thus must be memorized or researched in a dictionary or style book. Some verbs work both in the regular and irregular modes.

Drill 1:

1. burn   *burned*   *burned*
2. read   *read*   *read*
3. hear   *heared*   *heared*
4. talk   *talked*   *talked*
5. catch   *caught*   *caught*

Drill 2:

Write the infinitive predicate for the word in parentheses and write "R" for regular verb or "I" for irregular verb.

Example:

Martin (rang) _____ the bell at school for the recess period.

Martin (rang) _ring_ the bell at school for the recess period.

Ring = I

1. The housekeeper (had washed) *washed* Arnold's clothes, and accidentally (had shrunk) *shrink* his blue jeans.

2. Silvester (had dived) *dive* into the pool without first testing its depth.

3. Michaela (laid) *lay* the books on top of her desk after she (had read) *read I* thoroughly, and (had studied) *study R* every diagram.

4. The cat (sprang) *spring* like a coil when it saw a large mouse (lead) *lead* three other mice across the floor.

Drill 3:

Circle the verbs that are irregular.

(be)	(swing)	spy	transfer	(dig)	share
bill	act	(bind)	(bend)	(flee)	(sink)
hug	enter	occur	promise	(quit)	require
(lose)	smile	(cast)	suppose	indicate	talk

Modifiers
MISPLACED AND DANGLING MODIFIERS

Modifiers, which can be adjectives or adverbs, are words, phrases or clauses that describe. But when they are misplaced or used improperly, they create vagueness or ambiguity (uncertainty) about what the sentence is trying to say. Instead of describing the right words, misplaced or dangling modifiers cause the sentence's message to be unclear. **Misplaced modifiers** aren't positioned correctly in a sentence and thus create murkiness in meaning. Similar to misplaced modifiers are **dangling modifiers**, which fail to point to the proper words to be described because they dangle between clauses. Dangling modifiers may be located at the beginning of sentences as introductory clauses, and they can take on different forms such as <u>participial phrases</u>, <u>infinitive phrases</u>, <u>prepositional phrases</u>, and <u>elliptical clauses</u>. *"Squinting modifiers"* are also misplaced or dangling clauses.

SECTION 1:

Misplaced Modifiers

Misplaced modifiers don't point clearly to the word or phrases they intend to modify; often, they are placed in a part of the sentence that is unrelated to what should be modified, hence the term, "misplaced."

1. Limiting Modifiers

Players:

These types of misplaced modifiers include such words as those in this chart and are referred to as "limiting" because they limit or narrow the meaning of the words being modified.

only	nearly	just	even
almost	scarcely	often	merely
barely	exactly	hardly	simply

Rule Application:

Place the limiting modifier(s) directly in front of the word being modified. The entire meaning of a sentence can be changed by misplacing the modifier.

MODEL

Wrong: You will <u>only</u> need to ask one question.

Right: You will need to ask <u>only</u> one question.

Model Explanation:

The word being modified in the above example is *"question,"* not *"need."* By repositioning the misplaced modifier from *"only need"* to *"only one,"* the meaning of the sentence becomes clear so that we understand that it is only one question and not only a need.

2. Phrases and Clauses

How and where clauses and phrases are positioned in a sentence determine what gets modified, and, hence, what the sentence connotes.

MODEL

> **Wrong:** The speaker was said to be a heavy man wearing a gray toupee weighing more than 200 pounds.
>
> **Right:** The speaker was said to be a heavy man weighing more than 200 pounds, wearing a gray toupee.

Rule Application:

Position descriptive phrases and clauses nearest to the words being modified.

Model Explanation:

In the **wrong** statement, the misplaced descriptive phrase, *weighing more than 200 pounds*, mistakenly modifies the toupee instead of the man; hence, it sounds as though the hairpiece weighs 200 pounds. The **right** statement has the modifying phrase repositioned next to the word *"man"* so that readers understand that it is he who is 200 pounds, and not the toupee.

3. Lengthy Detours

Misplaced modifiers can occur by the placement of words and phrases between the subject and verb that creates a long route from the subject to the predicate; this is why this practice is referred to as "lengthy detour."

MODEL

> **Wrong:** Michael, after introducing everyone in the organization and then giving directions, left the room.
>
> **Right:** After introducing everyone in the organization and then giving directions, Michael left the room.

Rule Application:

Don't separate subject from verb by extra words, long phrases (lengthy detours), or clauses that split the connection in the fluidity of thought.

Model Explanation:

In the **wrong** example, the subject *"Michael"* is separated from the verb or predicate *"left"* by a series of words (a detour), and thus the meaning of the sentence gets lost in all those words. It's better to keep the subject and verb next to each other, as the **right** example demonstrates. Rewrite the sentence to achieve this.

SECTION 2:

Dangling Modifiers

Dangling modifiers are similar to misplaced modifiers, with the difference being that dangling descriptors don't seem to go anywhere (which is why they're referred to as "dangling") whereas misplaced ones do, even if they have been improperly aligned with the wrong words. There are essentially six types of dangling modifiers: **participial phrases, infinitive** phrases, **squinting modifiers, gerunds, elliptical phrases, prepositional/ adverb phrases.** Note: Some grammarians consider squinting modifiers as misplaced modifiers as well.

1. Participial Phrases

Introductory phrases (such as those using adjectives as descriptors) often end up dangling because the subject of the sentence doesn't logically follow. Proper participial phrases have a participle and an object, plus modifiers that describe a specific noun or pronoun.

Rule Application:

Adjectives or participial phrases must sensibly modify a subject following the phrase.

MODEL

Wrong: Giving up smoking, the nicotine no longer stained my fingers.

Right: When I gave up smoking, my fingers no longer had nicotine stains.

Model Explanation:

In the **wrong** statement, it sounds as though the _nicotine_ gave up smoking. The **right** sentence has a subject ("_I_") in its participial phrase that connects to the subject's ("_I_") _fingers;_ thus, we see that the person's fingers are no longer stained by the nicotine. Omitting the subject **I** creates a dangling modifier. Notice that to become grammatically correct, this sentence has been recast to include a proper subject.

2. Infinitive Phrases

Infinitive phrases contain the "_to_" word, as in "_to dance_" or "_to keep._" If this phrase doesn't properly modify the subject, the phrase will dangle.

Rule Application:

Do not split infinitives (separating the "_to_" from the verb); do not insert words between the "to" and the verb. Note that some grammarians today are more accepting of split infinitives, though it's a good idea to limit them.

MODEL

Wrong: To make sure all patients are properly treated, HMOs are coming under close scrutiny.

Right: To make sure all patients are properly treated, health investigators are closely scrutinizing HMOs.

Model Explanation:

The entire infinitive phrase, "_To make sure all patients are properly treated,_" dangles because it doesn't logically modify a subject. _HMOs_ cannot be the subject since they are inanimate and have no ability to perform action. But in the **right** example, we see that the infinitive phrase modifies the word _investigators_, which doesn't refer to an inanimate object. The incorrect sentence has been corrected by restructuring the modifying clause so that it describes a subject.

Separating the "to" from the verb by extra words also results in dangling infinitive phrases, as in: "_The coaching staff agreed to—before the first game of the season occurred—cut the team by ten players._" Here, the "_to_" is split from "_cut_" by a series of words. Always keep the infinitive phrase intact.

3. Gerunds

Gerunds are a part of speech that act as nouns and usually end in "_ing._"

MODEL

Wrong:	Driving to work, the roads seemed to have been newly paved.
Right:	Driving to work, I noticed that the roads seemed to have been newly paved.

Model Explanation:

The **wrong** example reads as though the roads were driving to work, which is illogical. Therefore, the sentence needs a subject (a "do-er") which should be **I** or some person that the gerund phrase can modify. Notice how the **right** statement reads better and makes more sense than the incorrect statement.

4. Adverb Phrases

Adverb phrases modify verbs, adjectives, and other adverbs, though they may also be prepositional phrases as well. If the adverb phrase fails to modify a verb, adjective, or another adverb properly, it dangles and needs to be corrected.

MODEL

Wrong:	With extraordinary strength, the muscle man moved the safe across the room.
Right:	The muscle man, with extraordinary strength, moved the safe across the room.

Model Explanation:

The phrase *with extraordinary strength* is a prepositional phrase (the word *"with"* is a preposition) acting as an adverb because it modifies the verb *moved*. But in the **wrong** example, the phrase dangles because it acts as an introductory clause, and, thus, fails to modify the proper word. By relocating the phrase next to the verb, the meaning of the sentence becomes clear.

Another example is *"That many college students today have taken up smoking, the tobacco officials noted in their report"* fails to modify a verb, adverb, or adjective. By recasting it to "The tobacco officials noted in their report that many college students today have taken up smoking," the sentence works because the adverb clause (beginning with *"that"*) properly modifies the verb "noted." Keep in mind that adverb clauses must describe verbs, adverbs, or adjectives.

5. Elliptical Clauses

These types of dangling modifiers result from absent information, such as missing verbs or missing subjects.

MODEL

Wrong:	When violent, meteorologists try to give television viewers early storm warnings.
Right:	When storms are predicted to be violent, meteorologists try to give television viewers early warnings.

Rule Application:

Gerunds, as nouns, may serve as subjects of sentences, but when they modify another part of a sentence, they need a subject to describe. It might be necessary to add selective words to a sentence to create a complete dependent clause that properly modifies the subject.

Rule Application:

When the flow of a sentence is interrupted by a dangling or misplaced clause, restructure the sentence by placing the phrase in its proper position.

Rule Application:

Supply the missing information in a sentence that has omitted a subject or verb in order to make the meaning clear and concise.

Model Explanation:

Elliptical clauses have something missing in them, as in the preceding model where there is no subject. In fact, without a topic, the sentence makes it sound as though meteorologists are violent, when the reference really applies to storms. By supplying the missing information (*"When storms are predicted to be violent"*), it's easy to understand the intent of the sentence. Notice that the key word is the subject *storms*; thus, it is the subject that is missing in this example. Also notice that the infinitive "to be" has remained intact, and not separated by extraneous words.

6. Squinting Modifiers

These types of dangling modifiers make for interesting sentences since what is being modified can be interpreted differently. Because of their ambiguous placement, squinting modifiers appear to modify either the word before it or the word following it.

Wrong: The employee Mrs. Brown scolded <u>angrily</u> quit his job.

Right: The employee Mrs. Brown <u>angrily</u> scolded quit his job.

Rule Application:

Move the modifier nearest to, and before, the word being modified to give clarity to the sentence.

Model Explanation:

In the **wrong** example, the sentence can be interpreted one of two ways: That Mrs. Brown scolded angrily, or that the employee angrily quit his job. In either case, the meaning is unclear. But by moving the modifier (*angrily*) before the verb or predicate ("*scolded*"), we understand that it is Mrs. Brown who was angry. Thus, the location of modifiers in a sentence determines how the meaning will be interpreted. Squinting modifiers are a common flaw in writing. Be on guard for them.

Summary

Modifiers dangle or are misplaced when they don't logically modify the intended words or phrases in a sentence; thus, such misplacement produces vagueness or ambiguity in meaning.

Misplaced modifiers are usually adjectives or adverbs, while dangling modifiers are often introductory clauses. Dangling modifiers can take the form of participial phrases, infinitive phrases, prepositional/adverb phrases, elliptical phrases, gerunds, and squinting modifiers.

Errors in placement of modifiers can be corrected by rewriting the sentence, filling in missing information, and/or placing modifiers next to the words they're attempting to modify.

Drill 1:

1. You will only need to read one book for the exam.

2. Getting out of my car, the college quad loomed before me.

3. After trying to make a western omelet, a cookbook was read for directions.

4. We had nearly driven a hundred miles when we realized we had left the coffee pot on.

5. While riding a trolley, a friend ran into her.

6. I have a couple of slices of apple pie that my mom baked in my lunch box.

7. Strumming your guitar lightly soothes me.

8. We enjoyed the autumn leaves walking along the path.

9. Walking over the hill, the valley lay in all its splendor.

10. Her brother often would come home.

Underline the word or phrases that are misplaced or dangle in these sentences. Recast the sentences that have these flaws.

Example:

Wrong: <u>Even though filled with hot peppers</u>, Bobby ate all the pizza.

Right: Bobby ate all the pizza even though it was filled with hot peppers.

Drill 2:

1. After looking at many cars on the dealership lot, the window labels have to be compared and discussed.

2. To understand the lab results, medical tests have to be clearly explained.

3. Passing the old cathedral, the beautiful stained-glass windows glistened and sparkled with deep, rich colors and designs.

4. When fierce and powerful storm chasers sometimes become just as afraid as lay people do.

5. Detailing the contract terms clearly helps to make the terms much easier to comprehend and negotiate.

Underline the misplaced or dangling modifiers; rewrite the sentences to read correctly, and determine the type of modifier in error.

Example:

Wrong: <u>Handing out detailed worksheets</u>, the math problems became better understood.

Right: <u>Handing out detailed worksheets</u> helps students to better understand the math problems. <u>participial phrase</u>

Prepositions and Case

One of the properties of nouns is **case**. Nouns have these cases: 1) Nominative or Subjective; 2) Objective or Accusative; and 3) Possessive (see next chapter). <u>Nominative</u> case is used as the subject of a verb, direct address, predicate pronoun and appositive. <u>Objective</u> is for direct and indirect objects, objects of a preposition, object complements, and subject of infinitives; they may be "reflexive." Pronouns also are an important aspect of case because they substitute for nouns and thus may also be nominative, objective, or possessive. Case works with **pronouns** and **prepositions**, as well as with appositives, and connects with gerunds. Case must be considered when forming agreement in number, person and gender. This chapter focuses on nominative and objective cases.

Part I: Objective Case

The objective case is used for direct objects, indirect objects, objects of prepositions, object complements, and the subjects of infinitives. This section looks at three main forms.

SECTION 1:

Prepositions and Their Objects

Prepositions connect nouns or pronouns with other words in the sentence. The noun or pronoun following the preposition is called the <u>object</u> of the preposition.

Players:

Here is a sampling of some common prepositions. Objective pronouns are also listed.

COMMON PREPOSITIONS		SAMPLE OBJECTIVE PRONOUNS		
of	in place of	his	himself	
in	considering	her	herself	
by	aboard	my	myself	
for	except	our	ourselves	REFLEXIVE
beneath	than	your	yourselves	
because of	as	me	itself	
in spite of	before	you	yourself	
after	behind	him	themselves	

like	down	her
during	with	it
upon	onto	us
outside	despite	them
from	regarding	their
throughout	toward	its
according to	to	whomever
until	at	mine
in addition to	around	whose
because	up	yours

> Reflexive pronouns reflect on the subject and can act as direct objects, indirect objects, and objects of a preposition.

MODEL

Wrong: "Those gifts are for her and I."

Right: "Those are for her and me."

Rule Application:

When pronouns follow prepositions, they should come from the objective case.

Model Explanation:

In applying the basic rule, the **wrong** pattern in model 1 makes use of two pronouns: *"her"* and *"I."* The pronoun *"her"* is correct because it follows the preposition *"for"* and is properly in objective case, which means the *"I"* should be changed to *"me."* The second pronoun, *"I,"* is incorrect because it belongs to a different category of pronouns called nominative, and can only be used as a *subject* of a sentence, or following a *linking verb*. The **right** pattern demonstrates the proper way to write pronouns following prepositions. Notice that both pronouns—not just one, as in *"her"* — must be in the objective case.

SECTION 2:

Direct Objects (DOs)

DOs are objects of subjects following predicates and belong to the objective case.

Players:

Here is a pattern showing how DOs are reflexive pronouns, and follow the predicate "saw."

	Subject	Predicate/Verb	**Direct Object**	Prep. Phrase
Example:	The puppy	saw	itself	in the mirror.

MODEL

Wrong: Our team beat they.

Right: Our team beat them.

Rule Application:

Use objective case for those pronouns and nouns acting as direct objects.

Model Explanation:

In the previous sentence, the word *"team"* is the subject; *"beat"* is the predicate; *"them"* is the correct direct object. Because *"them"* is in the direct object position, the pronoun used here must come from the objective case. *"They"* doesn't belong in the objective case (it's a nominative pronoun), but *"them"* does.

SECTION 3:

Indirect Objects (IOs)

Indirect objects (IOs) belong in the objective case.

Players:

Here is an example of a sentence with both an IO and a DO.

Subject	Predicate	Indirect Object	Direct Object
Sam	gave	himself	the largest piece of cake.

MODEL

Wrong: She offered he a list of toys for sale.

Right: She offered him a list of toys for sale.

Rule Application:

The objective case must be used when a pronoun is positioned as the indirect object.

Model Explanation:

An indirect object tells *"to whom"* or *"for whom,"* and indirectly receives the action of the verb. As an IO, its pronoun must be of the objective case. In the **wrong** example, *"he"* is a pronoun not listed as belonging to the objective case (it belongs to the nominative case), and thus is wrong. Instead, the pronoun *"him"* is needed, as shown in the **right** example.

Part II: Nominative Case

The nominative case is used when the pronoun is the subject of a **verb**, direct address, predicate noun and predicate pronoun; this section reviews subjects and predicates in the nominative case.

SECTION 1:

Subjects (S)

Pronouns can serve as subjects, and when they do, they must come from the nominative case.

Players:

Here are the pronouns belonging to the nominative case.

I	we	you	he	they	she	whoever	it

Rule Application:

When a pronoun serves as the subject of a sentence, it must belong to the nominative case.

M O D E L

Wrong: My sister and me   are going   shopping today.

Right: My sister and I   are going   shopping today.

Model Explanation:

In the above **right** example, the subject is a compound (*"My sister and I"*). Because *I* is part of the subject, it must come from the nominative case (also called "subjective" case). In the **wrong** statement, the pronoun *me* comes from the objective—not nominative—case, and thus is the incorrect word. If unsure of what the subject should be, delete each pronoun in a compound subject (in this case *"My sister"*), and read it accordingly. By doing that here, the sentence would erroneously read *"Me are going shopping today."* Since this is grammatically incorrect, it tells you that *"me"* must be replaced with *"I,"* which is nominative (see chart above under "players").

SECTION 2:

Predicate Nominative

The predicate nominative or predicate noun (PN) is one that is dependent upon the verb form and its placement in a sentence. Nouns used in this manner represent the subject.

M O D E L

Wrong: I know <u>whom</u> left the doors and windows closed.

Right: I know <u>who</u> left the doors and windows closed.

Rule Application:

A pronoun as the subject of a sentence is referred to as a <u>predicate nominative</u>, and thus must come from the nominative case.

Model Explanation:

Whom belongs to the objective case, not nominative, which makes the first statement **wrong**. *Who* is a pronoun belonging to the nominative case and, thus, is the **right** word. To determine when to use *"who"* and *"whom,"* consider that *"who"* corresponds to the nominative case, as do the pronouns *"he, she, they,"* with *"whom"* corresponding to the objective pronouns *"him, her, them."* Hence, substituting *"him"* in the wrong statement ("I know <u>him</u> left the doors. . ."), the sentence becomes grammatically incorrect. Try the nominative pronoun *"he"*: "I know <u>he</u> left the doors. . ." . This sounds correct, which tells you that the pronoun that must go in that spot has to come from the nominative case; therefore, <u>who</u> is the proper word.

M O D E L

Wrong: It was <u>them</u> who started the gang fight.

Right: It was <u>they</u> who started the gang fight.

Rule Application:

A linking verb can be key to determining when to use the nominative case for the predicate noun. Linking verbs (the verb form *"to be"*) require a predicate nominative (the nominative case).

Model Explanation:

The word <u>them</u> belongs to the objective case, not nominative. The key to what case is needed is seen in the predicate *"was"* which is a linking verb. Linking verbs (*"is," "are," "was," "were"*) require the nominative case. *They* belongs to the nominative case and, thus, is the right word.

Summary

The use of nominative and objective cases can be confusing in writing and speaking. Use the objective case (see chart in Part I) for the positions of direct object, indirect objects, and objects of prepositions. There are other instances when the objective case should be used but for our purposes here, the three positions mentioned above are sufficient to understanding the objective case.

Pronouns in the nominative case (see Part II) should be used when they serve as the subject or predicate nominative of a sentence, even though using this case after a linking verb may sound stilted. Pronouns may also be reflexive and emphatic in nature, as well as singular and plural. See Part I for insight into reflexive pronouns.

Drill 1:

In the blanks, write N if the information refers to the nominative case, and O if the information refers to the objective case.

Example:

Indirect objects = _O_ (objective case)

1. Direct objects = ___
2. Subjective case = ___
3. Predicate pronouns = ___
4. Prepositions = ___
5. Who, whoever = ___
6. Apposition = ___
7. Antecedents = ___
8. "himself," "itself" = ___
9. I, we, you, he... = ___
10. Indirect objects = ___

Drill 2:

Underline the correct objective or subjective pronouns.

Example:

We asked Mark and (she, _her_) to go with (we, _us_) to the concert.

1. "Between you and (I, me)," began the reporter, "you can reveal your source to (I, me)."

2. It is (me, I).

3. The teacher did call on both (she, her) and (I, me).

4. The alleged murderer claimed, "(Me, I) didn't kill (her, she)."

5. After (her, she) and (I, me) went Christmas shopping, (we, us) came home and made dinner for (they, them).

Drill 3:

1. He could see hisself in the mirror after he and her cleaned it.

2. Leave it up to I to get it wrong.

3. Ellie and me are going to the mall to pick them up at the theater.

4. Reading books is encouraged by we faculty members.

5. Marta's boyfriend treated her parents and she to dinner.

6. Everyone signed the birthday card except Elena and she.

7. Last summer Mr. Farnsworth hired Emily and I.

8. Both Miles and her have completely read the novel.

9. Fritz is a person who we all know.

10. I wonder whom will win the prize?

Replace the incorrect pronoun with the correct one.

Example:

<u>Him</u> and <u>me</u> are going to the show.

<u>He</u> and <u>I</u> are going to the show.

Possessives and Contractions

To create the **possessive** case, use the preposition "of" or add 's, or only the apostrophe ('), depending on the nature of the noun.

Possession shows ownership or origination, and may be shown with the "of" phrase ("the car <u>of</u> Mary") or by the insertion of an apostrophe ("Mary<u>'s</u> car"). Pronouns can also be used to show possession ("<u>her</u> car"). The possessive case is similar to the objective and nominative cases that we studied in Chapter 4 but here we concentrate on how to show ownership.

Contractions are often confused with possessives because both forms require apostrophes. Thus, this chapter also reviews contractions to indicate the differences.

Contractions blend two terms while omitting letters and inserting apostrophes, as in <u>was not</u> = <u>wasn't</u>. Contractions are not the same as possessive forms, although both look alike.

Part I: Possession

SECTION 1:

Showing Possession in Common Nouns

This section demonstrates how to show possession in some regular singular and plural nouns.

Players:

Here are three patterns for writing possession of nouns.

EXAMPLE 1: Apostrophes with singular nouns
SINGULAR NOUN + 'S = NOUN'S

EXAMPLE 2: Apostrophe with plural nouns
PLURAL NOUN + S' - NOUNS'

EXAMPLE 3: Use of the "of" phrase
THE NOUN + OF + OWNER

MODEL

Wrong: That books' page was ripped.

Right: That book's page was ripped.

Rule Application:

Use an apostrophe-s ('s) at the end of a singular noun to show ownership.

Model Explanation:

In the first statement, the word *books'* is wrong because the apostrophe after the "s" implies more than one book; yet, the verb *was* is singular. The **right** example indicates one book's page, and not several books.

MODEL

Wrong: Those book's pages were ripped.

Right: Those books' pages were ripped.

Rule Explanation:

To show possession in a plural-ized noun, add an *apostrophe (')* after the **s** that shows plurality.

Model Explanation:

In the **wrong** example, the word *book* improperly shows possession because the statement's intent is to indicate more than one book through the use of the word *"those,"* but an *'s* shows possession of only one item, so this is wrong. The **right** statement shows through the apostrophe (*s'*) that there is more than one book; since this possessive form is written by the addition of the *'*, it is correct.

MODEL

Wrong: The pages in the book <u>of</u> Mary's were ripped.

Right: The pages in the book <u>of</u> Mary were ripped.

Rule Application:

To show ownership without the use of an apostrophe, use the <u>of</u> phrase.

Model Explanation:

The **wrong** statement is redundant because the phrase *book of* already shows possession, so by writing Mary*'s*, it's similar to writing the phrase twice. The **right** example displays how to use the *of* phrase without being repetitive; notice that Mary has no apostrophe-*s*. Although using *of* to show possession is correct, it sounds awkward and can be confusing.

SECTION 2:

Showing Possession in Singular Nouns Ending in "S"

Some nouns end in "s" even though they are singular in nature. This section looks at ways to show possession in those kinds of nouns.

Players:

There are two patterns that can be used to show ownership.

EXAMPLE 1: Add only an apostrophe to the "s" at the end of the word:
NOUNS + ' = NOUNS'

EXAMPLE 2: Add an 's to the "s" at the end of the word:
NOUNS + 'S = NOUNS'S

Rule Application:

In a noun naturally ending in an "s," place the apostrophe after the "s" and not before, thus breaking up the word. Never place an apostrophe within a word.

Rule Application:

In singular nouns ending in "s" (such as James, Thomas, Des Moines, economics, gymnastics, St. Louis, congress, boss, and so on), you can show possession by adding an 's after the "s" in the name, as in the first **acceptable** statement, or you can add only the ', as indicated in the second **acceptable** statement. Some conventional grammarians claim that adding only the ' after a singular word ending in "s" is the sole proper form, while others claim the addition of the 's for singular nouns is also acceptable. A way to decide is to determine if the word is hard to pronounce with the additional 's. For example, the possessive, "Illinois's" is difficult to pronounce, so it's better to go with "Illinois'"—adding the apostrophe only. Refer to a style book for help.

Rule Application:

Plural nouns ending in "s" require only an apostrophe at the end to show ownership.

MODEL

Wrong:	Thoma's coach was a former Steeler fullback.
Right:	Thomas' coach was a former steeler fullback.

Model Explanation:

The name _Thomas_ ends in an "s" which should be kept intact with the entire word; splitting the word by placing an apostrophe between the letters "a" and "s" is incorrect. The **right** statement shows how to properly create ownership in the name. Notice the apostrophe comes after the final "s" in the name.

MODEL

Acceptable:	Jesus's disciples followed Him everywhere.
Acceptable:	Jesus' disciples followed Him everywhere.

SECTION 3:

Showing Possession in Plural Nouns Ending in "S"

Unlike singular nouns (see above) ending in "s" where either an 's or just the ' can be added to show ownership, plural nouns ending in an "s" take only an ' at the end.

Players:

Here is the pattern for creating possession in plural nouns, with examples of plural nouns.

EXAMPLE 1: Pattern for showing possession
PLURAL NOUN (WITH s) + ' = NOUN WITH S'

EXAMPLE 2:		Sample plural nouns
agencies	=	agencies'
teachers	=	teachers'
years	=	years'
attorneys	=	attorneys'

MODEL

Wrong:	The goddesses's flowing gowns made them look angelic.
Right:	The goddesses' flowing gowns made them look angelic.

Model Explanation:

The word _goddesses_ is the plural of the word goddess (more than one goddess). Since the plural ends in an "s," only an apostrophe—not an 's—is needed to show ownership. Thus, in the above model, the second example is correct.

SECTION 4:

Showing Possession in Irregular Plural Nouns without "S"

Some nouns construct their plurality by changing their form (such as children) and not adding "s" to the end of their word. These kinds of words develop ownership simply by adding an 's.

Players:

Here is the pattern for creating possession in words that change form to construct plurality. A few examples of these types of words are given below

EXAMPLE 1: Pattern for showing possession
PLURAL NOUN + 'S = NOUN'S

EXAMPLE 2: Samples of a few such type of plural nouns

oxen	=	oxen's
geese	=	geese's
mice	=	mice's
women	=	women's

MODEL

Wrong: The alumnis' guest speaker was the governor.

Right: The alumni's guest speaker was the governor.

Model Explanation:

Because the word _alumni_ shows plurality through change in form and not through the addition of an "s," it is an irregular plural noun that requires the 's to show possession. Thus the first statement in the example is **wrong** because it places the apostrophe after the "s" when the word shouldn't have an "s" to indicate more than one alumnus (the plural of alumnus is _alumni_, without an "s"). The **right** sentence creates possession by adding an 's after the plural word _alumni_.

Rule Application:

Irregular nouns not ending in "s" fashion their plurality by changing form, and require an apostrophe "s" at the end of their irregular form.

SECTION 5:

Showing Possession of Compound Words or Word Groups

Constructing possessions in compound words can be a little tricky. Here are some ideas.

Players:

Below is the basic pattern for creating possessive form in compound words; a list of sample compound words is given.

EXAMPLE 1: COMPOUND NOUN + 'S = COMPOUND NOUN'S

EXAMPLE 2: SAMPLE COMPOUND NOUNS AND THEIR POSSES-SIVES

mother-in-law	=	mother-in-law's
lieutenant general	=	lieutenant general's
senator-elect	=	senator-elect's
runner-up	=	runner-up's

MODEL

Wrong: The mother's-in-law briefcase is black leather.

Right: The mother-in-law's briefcase is black leather.

Rule Application:

Add an apostrophe "s" only to the final element of a compound noun or group of words to form the possessive; do not add the 's to the root element, as in the **wrong** statement.

Model Explanation:

The final element in the singular compound word *"mother-in-law"* is the word *"law,"* which gets the apostrophe "s," not the root or main word _mother_. If uncertain about how to make a compound word possessive, refer to a style book.

SECTION 6:

Showing Possessions in Individual and Joint Words

When two names own something, creating possession is based on whether the two show individual or joint ownership.

Players:

Below are two ways to create possession for more than one person.

EXAMPLE 1: Individual ownership of a party of two
NOUN + 'S + NOUN + 'S = NOUN'S + NOUN'S

EXAMPLE 2: Joint ownership of a party of two
NOUN + NOUN + 'S = NOUN + NOUN'S

EXAMPLE 3: INDIVIDUAL ownership by two or more

Mark and Harry	=	Mark's and Harry's
Chrysler and Mercury	=	Chrysler's and Mercury's
faculty and principal	=	faculty's and principal's

JOINT ownership by two or more

Proctor & Gamble	=	Proctor & Gamble's
king and queen	=	king and queen's
parent and student	=	parent and student's

Rule Application:

Place an **'s** after each name in a sentence that appears to have individual ownership.

MODEL

Wrong: Mark and Harry's pictures appeared in the newspaper.

Right: Mark's and Harry's pictures appeared in the newspaper.

Model Explanation:

Both Mark and Harry have pictures of themselves in the newspapers; thus, each must show possession. By putting an 's after the name _Mark_ and the name _Harry_, each shows ownership of their own photos.

> **MODEL**
>
> **Wrong:**   Proctor's & Gamble's ad campaign brought in many consumers.
>
> **Right:**   Proctor & Gamble's ad campaign brought in many consumers.

Rule Application:

When nouns show joint owner-ship, place the apostrophe "s" after the last noun only.

Model Explanation:

The nouns _Proctor & Gamble_ show joint ownership. Only the final name receives the apostrophe since they both act as one unit; therefore, the second statement in the model is **right**.

SECTION 7:

Showing Possession through Pronouns

The following words are pronouns that show possession.

Players:

These words don't require an apostrophe "s." Indefinite pronouns do require an apostrophe-s ('s) after their final consonant.

PERSONAL PRONOUNS		INDEFINITE PRONOUNS	
Singular	**Plural**	anybody's	no one's
his	their/theirs	anyone's	somebody's
her/hers	their/theirs	everybody's	someone's
my/mine	our/ours	everyone's	
your/yours	your/yours	nobody's	
its			

> **MODEL**
>
> **Wrong:**   This is her's computer.
>
> **Right:**   This is her computer.

Rule Application:

To make pronouns show owner-ship, use the possessive form above by referring to the chart.

Model Explanation:

Because the word _her_ already indicates possession, an apostrophe "s" isn't needed for the personal pronouns, although they are required for the indefinite pronouns in showing ownership. Thus, the first statement is **wrong** because it adds an apostrophe "s" to a pronoun that, by nature, is already possessive.

Rule Application:

Add an apostrophe "s" at the end of an indefinite pronoun that is singular in nature.

MODEL

Wrong: Is this anyones's coat?

Right: Is this anyone's coat?

Model Explanation:

Indefinite pronouns don't show ownership in their native form, as do personal pronouns. Thus, the apostrophe "s" must be added to the singular form, as demonstrated in the **right** statement of the model.

Part II: Contractions vs. Possessions

Contractions are similar to words using apostrophes, and thus they're easily confused.

Players:

Here is an incomplete list showing the differences between possessive forms and contractions.

CONTRACTIONS		POSSESSIVES	
Root Form	Contracted form	Item + Owner	Possessive Form
I am	I'm	book of Bob	Bob's book
you are	you're	fur of cat	cat's fur
we are	we're	prey of bird	bird's prey
she is/she has	she's	playground of kid	kid's playground
I would/I had	I'd	collar of dog	dog's collar

Rule Application:

To show ownership through the use of a pronoun, omit the apostrophe. To use a contracted form, delete the letter ("s"), and add an apostrophe.

MODEL

Wrong: Its up to her to pass her's exam.

Right: It's up to her to pass her exam.

Model Explanation:

In the first statement, the word *Its* is used as a pronoun when it should serve as the subject and verb (*it* [subject] and *is* [verb]). Thus *It's* (the contracted form) is needed. Also, the word *her's* is **wrong** since personal pronouns don't take an apostrophe "s" ('s).

Summary

Contractions serve as a shortcut for writing the subject and predicate as one through the blending of the person and the predicate, as in "I" (subject) + "have" (predicate/verb) = "I've." Contractions use an apostrophe just as possessives do, but possessives show ownership while contractions blend person with verb. Possessives may also show ownership through the use of the word "of" phrase (as in "the purse _of_ Melissa") when the use of an apostrophe makes the phrase difficult to say.

Drill 1:

Write the possessive and con-tractive form of each of the words below.

Example:

book = book's

Example:

children = children's

1. attorney = _____

2. boxes = _____

3. addresses = _____

4. oxen = _____

5. mother-in-law = _____

6. his = _____

7. House of Hayes = _____

8. attorney of defendant = _____

9. Mark and Henry (joint ownership) = _____

10. parties = _____

Drill 2:

Make possessive, then pluralize or singularize each word and phrase.

Example:

toys of the baby = baby's toys = babies' toys

Example:

case of the tools = tool's case = tools' case

1. at arm's length = _____ = _____

2. dogs' paws = _____ = _____

3. art work of Marcus = _____ = _____

4. club of the men = _____ = _____

5. ox's yolk = _____ = _____

Drill 3:

Correct the errors of possession and contractions in the following sentences. Place a "C" for "Correct" in the blank.

Example:
pant's zipper = pants' zipper
it tis = it's or it is

1. the sheeps' herd = _____   2. its noon = _____

3. Jim can't not = _____   4. toes' nails = _____

5. monkeys' back = _____   6. that's life = _____

7. a hero's welcome = _____   8. they's going = _____

9. employees' wages = _____   10. glass's frame = _____

Plurals

GENERAL RULE:

In most cases, a word can be pluralized by adding an "s" to it; in other instances, such as when a word ends in a "y," the suffix must be changed to "ies." Other situations require a complete change in word form or letter. In various conditions, a word may be singular or plural in the same form. See below for examples.

Plural means more than one person or thing; it's often referred to as "plurality." In order to pluralize some words, they may need to change form, although the letter "s" at the end of a word usually indicates plurality. This tells readers whether whatever is being referred to is a singular person or item, or more than one. When a subject in a sentence is pluralized, its verb or predicate must also reflect that plurality through agreement.

SECTION 1:

Forming Plurality of Common Words

Creating plurality involves no more than adding an "s" or "es" to the suffix.

Players:

Below are a few examples of words that become plural by adding "s" or "es."

SINGULAR FORM	PLURAL FORM
cat	cats
hero	heroes
house	houses
box	boxes
kiss	kisses
volcano	volcanoes
attorney	attorneys
snake	snakes
glass	glasses
taxi	taxis

Rule Application:

Most words can be pluralized by adding an "s" or an "es."

MODEL

Wrong: The racing <u>cars</u> had reached two <u>plateaues</u> before their <u>engine</u> stopped.

Right: The racing <u>cars</u> had reached two <u>plateaus</u> before their <u>engines</u> stopped.

Model Explanation:

In the **wrong** statement, the word <u>plateaus</u> is spelled incorrectly; only an "s" (not an "es") needs to be added. Likewise, the word <u>engine</u> must be pluralized because there's more than one car and, hence, more than one engine. The word <u>cars</u> is pluralized properly.

SECTION 2:

Forming Plurality in Words Ending in "Y" or "F"

Players:

The words in this chart end in a "y" or "f" and thus slightly change form when pluralized.

SINGULAR FORM	PLURAL FORM
wolf	wolves
baby	babies
party	parties
gallery	galleries
life	lives
roof	roofs

MODEL

Wrong: Chan picked <u>daisys</u> for Ling but she wanted <u>irisses</u>, though she put the <u>daisies</u> on the top two <u>shelfs</u>.

Right: Chan picked <u>daisies</u> for Ling but she wanted <u>irises</u>, though she put the <u>daisies</u> on the top two <u>shelves</u>.

Rule Application:

Nouns ending in "y" preceded by a consonant are pluralized by changing the "y" to "i" and adding "es."

Model Explanation:

The word <u>daisy</u> ends in a "y" and is preceded by the consonant "s" which means the "ies" form is needed to pluralize it. Also incorrect is the word <u>irisses</u> which needs only an "es" since it already ends in an "s." <u>Shelf</u> ends in an "f" and thus needs "ves" to make it plural; therefore, the word should be <u>shelves</u> instead of <u>shelfs</u>. Words ending in "fe" or "ff" may require only an "s" (as in "roofs") or "es" or the change to "ves." Check a dictionary to be on the safe side.

SECTION 3:

Forming Plurality of Irregular Words

Players:

The following words form plurality by changing their endings that may or may not take an "s."

SINGULAR FORM	PLURAL FORM
thesis	theses
bacterium	bacteria
stratum	strata
crisis	crises
woman	women
nucleus	nuclei
foot	feet
phenomenon	phenomena
focus	foci
goose	geese
ox	oxen

Rule Explanation:

Irregular nouns have their own form when pluralized, usually through the changing of the ending to an "a," or substituting an "e" for "i" as in thesis→ theses, or other unique forms. To ascertain what the form becomes, refer to a dictionary to be sure.

MODEL

Wrong: The <u>criterion</u> for the labeling of an event as a <u>phenomena</u> were several but only one single <u>data</u> fits the two <u>thesis</u> the scientists assigned in their set of <u>hypothesis</u>.

Right: The <u>criteria</u> for the labeling of an event as a <u>phenomenon</u> were several but only one single <u>datum</u> fits the two <u>theses</u> the scientists assigned in their set of <u>hypotheses</u>.

Model Explanation:

The plural of the word <u>criterion</u> is <u>criteria</u>, meaning more than one factor or measurement; and since the verb in the sentence is "were," which is plural, we understand that <u>criterion</u> needs to be pluralized to <u>criteria</u>, as in the **right** statement. <u>Phenomena</u> is the reverse in that it should be singular to <u>phenomenon</u> since it refers to only one event. <u>Data</u> should also be singularized to <u>datum</u> because the reference is to one element, though some grammarians accept <u>data</u> as plural and singular. The sentence discusses two (more than) "thesis," which then has to be pluralized to <u>theses</u>. Notice the change in spelling from "t-h-e-s-<u>i</u>-s" to "t-h-e-s-<u>e</u>-s." This is also true for the word "hypothesis" which is singular, but since the sentence refers to a set, the word **hypothesis** has to be pluralized to <u>hypotheses</u>, with the "e" after and before the "s".

SECTION 4:

Words That Remain Singular

Some words may look plural in appearance because of their final "s," but by nature they're singular and should take a singular verb. Notice that many of these words end in "ics."

Players:

Here is a sampling of words that are and remain singular in nature.

SINGULAR FORM ONLY

athletics	mathematics	trash
ethics	politics	bionics
luck	intelligence	clothing
electronics	pride	statistics
news	music	physics
wheat	economics	gymnastics
measles	summons	measles

Exception: When words ending in "ics" are used as a field of study, they're singular in nature, but when they refer to activities, they're considered plural, and thus take a plural predicate, such as in "Statistics indicate that there are more women in the world than there are men."

MODEL

Wrong: Sandy first tried taking up <u>mathematic</u> in college, but then she gave that up and tried majoring in <u>economic</u>; now <u>physics</u> are her major.

Right: Sandy first tried taking up <u>mathematics</u> in college, but then she gave that up and tried majoring in <u>economics</u>; now <u>physics</u> is her major.

Rule Application:

Some nouns retain their singularity whether or not they end in an "s." These words require singular predicates as well.

Model Explanation:

The word <u>mathematics</u> must have the letter "s" at the end since there is no such word as <u>mathematic</u>. The same is true for the word <u>economics</u>; the "'s" must remain on the word even though the word implies singularity. The word <u>physics</u> is singular, and thus requires a singular predicate—not the plural predicate "are."

SECTION 5:

Nouns That Remain Plural

This section deals with nouns that retain plurality even though reference may be made to only one of its kind.

Players:

Here is a sampling of words that stay plural no matter how they are used.

PLURAL FORM ONLY

scissors	jeans	grounds
pants	pincers	tweezers
barracks	riches	odds
trousers	goods	earnings
slacks	savings	credentials
thanks	belongings	eyeglasses
pliers	species	people
assets	premises	proceeds
winnings	leavings	quarters

Exception: The nouns trousers, pants, scissors, glasses, and pliers are always plural and are often preceded by the phrase "a pair of."

Rule Application:

Certain nouns as those featured in the previous chart retain their plurality regardless of how they're used in a sentence; hence, each of these nouns requires a plural verb for agreement between subject and predicate.

MODEL

Wrong: The <u>pliers</u> is used to bend wire.

Right: The <u>pliers</u> are used to bend wire.

Model Explanation:

The word *pliers* is plural whether it refers to one pair or many pairs. Therefore, such a word must also have a plural verb.

SECTION 6:

Nouns That Can Be Singular or Plural

There are a few nouns that can serve as singular or plural subjects; this section looks at some of them and how they interact with their predicates.

Players:

This chart represents a few of the nouns that can be singular or plural

sheep	fish	trout
quail	series	deer
species	means	series
moose	chassis	corps
gross		

Rule Application:

Nouns that act as singular subjects take singular predicates; when they behave as plural subjects, they require plural verbs.

MODEL

Wrong: There <u>is</u> several <u>deer</u> on the road.

Right: There <u>are</u> several <u>deer</u> on the road.

Model Explanation:

The first statement is wrong because it refers to more than one deer, and thus the subject is plural and requires a plural verb, as given in the **right** example.

SECTION 7:

Compound Words with More Than One Plural Form

Some compound words (two words that act as one) can be pluralized more than one way.

Players:

This chart illustrates a few compound words that can be pluralized different ways.

ONE FORM	ALTERNATE FORM
court martials	courts martial
notaries public	notary publics
attorneys general	attorney generals

Rule Application:

Those compound words that can be pluralized more than one way take plural verbs.

MODEL

Right: All the <u>notary publics</u> were located uptown.

Right: All the <u>notaries public</u> were located uptown.

Model Application:

In the above examples, notice that both statements are correct even though they're written differently. Always check the dictionary for what is grammatically acceptable.

SECTION 8:

Compound Words Forming Plurals at Main Word

Many compound words form their plurals by changing only the main word, or by adding an "s" to the ending of the word.

Players:

Here is a brief sampling of hyphenated words that are pluralized by altering their root or main word, or by adding an "s" at the suffix.

HYPHENATED WORD	PLURAL FORM
editor-in-chief	editor<u>s</u>-in-chief
man-of-war	m<u>e</u>n-of-war
lady-in-waiting	lad<u>ies</u>-in-waiting
writer-in-residence	writer<u>s</u>-in-residence
mother-in-law	mother<u>s</u>-in-law
commander-in-chief	commander<u>s</u>-in-chief
passer-by (passerby)	passer<u>s</u>-by (passer<u>s</u>by)
attorney-at-law	attorney<u>s</u>-at-law
vice-president	vice-president<u>s</u>
grant-in-aid	grant<u>s</u>-in-aid
justice-of-the-peace	justice<u>s</u>-of-the-peace
workman	workm<u>e</u>n
lineman	linem<u>e</u>n
grandchild	grandchild<u>re</u>n

MODEL

Wrong: The publisher held a meeting for all her <u>editor-in-chieves.</u>

Right: The publisher held a meeting for all her <u>editors-in-chief.</u>

Rule Application:

Refer to a dictionary to determine how to pluralize a hyphenated or compound word. Generally, plurality of these words follow the rules for the same words when not in compound form or when not hyphenated.

Model Explanation:

Since the word <u>*chief*</u> is not the main or root word, it shouldn't be pluralized; additionally, <u>*chiefs*</u> is the more acceptable plurality of <u>chief</u> anyway. However, since <u>*editor*</u> is the root or main word in the hyphenated form, it should be pluralized.

Notice that those compound words that form their plurality in regular usage by changing a letter (such as _man_ to _men_) follow this same pattern in compound words (_workman_ to _workmen_).

Collective Nouns As Singular or Plural Subjects

Collective nouns are words that represent a group, and can be plural or singular in nature. (See Chapter 1 for additional input on this topic.)

Players:

Here is list of some common collective nouns.

COLLECTIVE NOUNS

crowd	audience	kind
public	class	sort
family	band	number
group	team	jury
herd	committee	panel
gaggle	board	cartel
lot	dozen	department
staff	ton	squad
union	club	organization
cast	heap	pile
load	stack	mass
cluster	lump	league
lodge	family	coalition
guild	council	rally
mob	conclave	cabinet
congress	synod	swarm
throng	horde	multitude
assembly	convention	meeting
genre	caste	gathering
crew	bunch	circle
clique	league	administration
society	company	school
army	corporation	firm
majority	minority	flock

Rule Application:

Collective nouns receive singular verbs when they are thought of acting as one group, but when the noun connotes the activities of individual members in the group, the subject takes a plural verb. Thus, if the subject acts in the singular or as a unit, it must take a singular verb; likewise, if it behaves in the plural, it must take a plural verb.

MODEL

Wrong: I hope your <u>family are doing</u> well.

Right: I hope all the members of your <u>family are doing</u> well.

Model Explanation:

In the **wrong** example, the word _family_ acts as one unit, but in the second example, the individual members of the _family_ are referred to, so the subject takes a plural verb. When in doubt, ask yourself if the intent of the sentence means one unit or several in the unit. More than one will require a plural predicate.

Plurality and Singularity of Pronouns

(See Chapter One for additional information.)

Use these guidelines to help determine which pronouns are plural and which are singular; there are exceptions.

Singular Indefinite Pronouns						
each	every	either	neither	one	another	much

Singular Compound Pronouns					
anybody	anything	anyone	everybody	everything	everyone
somebody	something	someone	nobody	nothing	no one

Plural Indefinite Pronouns				
both	few	others	several	many

Singular/Plural Pronouns					
all	more	most	some	any	none

Summary

Plurals of nouns are formed in many different ways, depending on the word and its use in context. The simplest way to create a plural is by adding "s" or "es" to a noun's suffix; however, several types of nouns don't lend themselves to this, such as words ending in "y" or "f." In other cases, the word's ending may change entirely, as in "criterion" to "criteria."

Too, there are words that always remain plural no matter how they are used, such as "odds," while the opposite is also true, as in "news." Still, there are other words that can be plural or singular, e.g., "deer," and some words alter their endings or the letters inside the endings to form plurality ("woman" to "women"); this is also true for hyphenated and compound words ("editors-in-chief").

Collective nouns represent one unit referring to several people with a common cause, as seen in such words as "gang," "syndicate," and so on. Generally, collective nouns act singular and thus take a singular verb but if the members of the group act individually, the collective noun takes a plural verb.

Write the plural in the blank next to the singular word.

Example:

match _____

match _matches_

Drill 1:

1. mouse = _____   6. scissors = _____

2. deer =   _____   7. alumnus = _____

3. bus =   _____   8. loaf =   _____

4. nucleus = _____   9. pharmacy = _____

5. pants =   _____   10. oasis =   _____

Give the plurals of the words in bold.

Example:

The **basis** _____ for studying **fungus** _____ is to learn about non-chlorophyll **growth** _____.

The **basis** _bases_ for studying **fungus** _fungi_ is to learn about non- chlorophyll **growth** _growth_.

Drill 2:

1. The **faculty** _____ is _____ **alumnae** _____ of the all-women's college.

2. The **committee** _____ thinks _____ the **jury** _____ will soon return.

3. The **town's** _____ **sheriff** _____ said the **attorney** _____ claimed the **murder** _____ **was** _____ done with the **knife** _____.

4. The **product** _____ **works** _____ by neutralizing the **particle** _____ that **is** _____ trapped in the **upholstery** _____.

5. **My** _____ **company** _____ **is** _____ located near the **river's** _____ bank.

Active and Passive Voice

The voice and strength of a sentence are determined by the predicate (verb and verb phrase). Verbs can make a sentence strong (**active**) or weak (**passive**), depending on whether they're transitive or intransitive, and how they're used in a sentence. This section looks at the use of active and passive voice. Active voice is generally preferred over passive voice because "active" shows action and empowers writing.

Part I: Overview of Voice

Active voice relies on the use of transitive verbs—verbs that aren't linking or auxiliary. While <u>**subject complements**</u> are associated with **passive voice**, <u>**object complements**</u> are related to **active voice**.

MODEL		
Transitive/DO	Fire destroyed the documents. **ACTIVE**
Intransitive/no DO	The documents were destroyed by fire. **PASSIVE**

Model Explanation:

In the first statement (**transitive**), *fire* is the subject, <u>destroyed</u> is the active verb, and <u>documents</u> is the **direct object** that indicates the person or thing receiving the action. The transitive verb, <u>destroyed</u>, has the subject as the "*doer*" of the sentence while the receiver of the action is the direct object. In the **intransitive** sentence, the linking verb ("*were*") has the subject receiving the action instead of performing it; thus it is passive in voice. Notice how more dynamic the sentence sounds in active voice.

Part II: Object Complements

A complement completes the verb or predicate in a sentence. Object complements can be adjectives, nouns, or groups of words. They may come in three forms: 1) direct objects; 2) indirect object; 3) object of a preposition.

GENERAL RULE:

To make a sentence active, move the object to the subject's position. To make a sentence passive, move the subject to the object's position and use linking verbs.

Rule Application:

To make a sentence active (transitive), use strong verbs with object complements such as direct objects, which act as recipients of subjects.

SECTION 1:

Direct Object

The direct object is the word that receives the action of a transitive verb.

Players:

Here is the basic model of a sentence in active voice with a direct object

S	V (predicate)	DO (direct object)
Snow	blanketed	the city.

Rule Application:

Direct objects designate who or what receives the action. They make the sentence stronger, and thus create lively writing through the active voice. In most instances, use the active voice via transitive verbs.

MODEL

Wrong: The ball was thrown by Bobby.

Right: Bobby threw the ball.

Model Explanation:

S	V	DO
Bobby	threw	the ball.

In the **wrong** example (*intransitive*) the message comes across as weak because the subject of the sentence, _ball,_ performs no action; it's not a "*do-er.*" But if _Bobby_ is made the subject and the "*doer,*" the sentence comes alive and delivers a stronger message. Thus, by making _Bobby_ the subject and changing the verb (predicate) to active voice (_threw_), the meaning is empowered. Notice that in the **right** example (*transitive*), the direct object is _ball_.

SECTION 2:

Object of Preposition

MODEL

	passive	S	V (predicate)	prep	object of preposition
Obj. Prep:		The ball was thrown		by	Bobby.

	active	S	V	DO
DO:		Bobby threw		the ball.

Model Explanation:

The intransitive or passive version comes across as weak because the subject performs no action, and _Bobby_ has the action performed on him, instead of by him. In this case, _Bobby,_ as the receiver of the action, is called _the object of the preposition_ because the word "*by*" is the preposition. The linking verb "*was*" makes the sentence intransitive or passive, and thus weakens the writing.

SECTION 3:

Indirect Object

Indirect objects precede direct objects and tell for whom the action occurs.

Players:

Here is the basic model for the placement of the indirect object.

S	V	(IO) Indirect Object	DO
Liz	gave	Romolo	the playbill.

MODEL

No IO: I wrote a brief note.

With IO: I wrote my cousin a brief note.

Rule Application:

Nouns that come before direct objects are called indirect objects. Use them to tell for whom or to whom the action is being performed.

Model Explanation:

The **No IO** example has no *indirect object*, although it does have a **direct object**. In this sentence, *I* is the **subject**, *wrote* is the **verb** or **predicate**, and *note* is the **direct object**. There is no indirect object that should come before the direct object. The **With IO** sentence demonstrates the use of an indirect object through the word *cousin*, which is *to whom* the note is written. The word *note* remains as the direct object.

SECTION 4:

Passive Voice

Passive voice weakens a sentence. Because the subject is acted upon instead of doing the action, there is no power to the words. Although passive voice weakens the words in a sentence, here are examples when it can be useful: 1) to avoid calling attention to the "doer" of the action; 2) to emphasize the receiver of the action instead of the "doer". Passive voice generally relies on intransitive verbs. There are other times when passive voice is preferred, such as to add variety to sentence structures as well as serving as smooth transitions. Unless there are specific reasons for wanting to use the passive voice, it's best to write in the active mode.

Players:

Helping or auxiliary verbs (verbs that cannot be used independently) and linking verbs ("to be" form) create passive voice in writing. This chart lists some of those verbs

COMMON AUXILIARY	LINKING VERBS		MODAL AUXILIARY	
to be	seem	appear	will	need
to have	being	smell	may	might
to do	were	become	dare	must
am	grow	prove	can	ought (to)
was	turn	feel	may	shall
are	need	remain		

SECTION 5:

Subject Complements

Subject complements can be **predicate nominatives or nouns**, or **predicate adjectives**. The model below gives an example of each.

Rule Application:

A noun following a linking verb is referred to as a predicate noun or predicate nominative, and makes the sentence passive and intransitive. An adjective that follows a linking verb is called a predicate adjective and is also passive.

M O D E L

Predicate Nominative:
S   V   PN (predicate noun/nominative)
I am a <u>professor</u>.

Predicate Adjective:
S   V   PA (predicate adjective)
I am tired.

Model Explanation:

Passive voice has a *subject complement*, which can be a **predicate nominative/noun** (*I am <u>boss</u>*), or a **predicate adjective** (*I am not <u>old</u>*). The predicate nominative/noun has a noun as the receiver of the action, while the predicate adjective has an adjective as the receiver. To eliminate passive voice, avoid the use of linking and auxiliary verbs.

Summary

In most cases, active voice is preferred over passive voice because it is less wordy and shows action. Passive voice may be used for smooth transitions, when the receiver of the action is more important than the "doer" of the action, and when a writer wants to avoid calling attention to the performer of the action. Active voice requires a powerful, nonlinking verb where the subject is performing the action.

Underline any verbs (if present) that make the sentence passive. Tell whether the verb you indicated is linking or auxiliary.

Example:

Mary remained angry.

(Answer: <u>remained</u>—linking)

Drill 1:

1. Jimmy became old enough to drive.

2. I can do jigsaw puzzles in a short period of time.

3. The roses smelled fresh and aromatic.

4. Marcia skipped all the way home.

5. Banks seem to be helpful regarding money management.

6. The jitterbug was my grandmother's favorite dance.

7. Retail stores sell their products on the internet these days.

8. I may need a cup of coffee to steady my nerves.

Drill 2:

Use sentences from Drill 1.

Substitute active verbs for passive in above sentences. Answers will vary.

Example:

Mary <u>remained</u> angrily. (Mary <u>acted</u> angrily.)

Drill 3:

1. Louis says Y2K is the term for the computer problem predicted for the year 2000.

2. Marta appears mature in her prom picture.

3. Give Charissa a smile.

4. Brynne is the president of her high school senior class.

5. She is exhausted.

6. You are relieved of your duty.

7. I relieve you of your duty.

8. He sent her a present of roses.

9. The package had been placed in the garage.

10. The child was bitten on the arm by the raccoon.

11. Cecily hit a home run during the game.

12. My friend has remodeled the house near ours.

13. The wind blew a large tree into the powerlines.

14. Every new book has been shelved.

15. The audience was amused.

Label the parts of the following sentences by using these designations:

DO = direct object ; PN = predicate noun/nominative; PA = predicate adjective; OP= object of a preposition; IO = indirect object; SC = subject complement; S = subject; V = verb. Indicate whether the sentence is active or passive.

Example:
S   V   IO
Experts told the Arctic researchers
            OP
about a major blizzard.
(active voice)

Example:
S   V PA
You look fine. (passive voice)

The Articles "An" and "A"

The articles "a" and "an" are only used with singular nouns or if there is an adjective before the noun. Pronunciation of the noun determines what article to use.

Only a few words in the English language pose real problems to the writer when using the article "an." Primarily, they are words that begin with 'h" which is silent, 'o" which can sound like the consonant "w", and "u" or "eu" which can sound like the consonant "y." The rule usually followed ("a" before consonants and "an" before vowels) does not apply to these exceptions.

Players:

This chart shows a sampling of problem words for using "an" and "a."

SAMPLE WORD			"AN" OR "A" USAGE
European	a	eucalyptus	a
eulogy	a	euphoric	a
hedgehog	a	hot (summer)	a
hour	an	historical (event)	a
history (lesson)	a	holiday	a
horrible	a	honor(able)	an
Italian	an	jalapeno	a
once (in a lifetime)	a	ukelele	a
Ukranian	a	Ulysses (drama)	a
umbrella	an	unified	a
uniform	a	unit	a

Rule Application:

Usually, the article "an" precedes a vowel, while generally the indefinite article "a" goes before a consonant.

MODEL

Wrong: The teacher walked into the boardroom a hour late

Right: The teacher walked into the boardroom an hour late

Model Explanation:

The word "hour" (pronounced *our*) begins with an "h," a consonant which is silent during speech. Because it sounds as though it begins with a vowel, this word is preceded by "an."

MODEL

Wrong: Olivia St. Forbes is an European.

Right: Olivia St. Forbes is a European.

The indefinite article "a" should be used before the letters "u" and "eu" when they sound like the word "you."

Model Explanation:

Although the article *"an"* usually precedes a vowel (such as in "an" octopus), the above model represents an exception to the rule because the *"eu"* in European sounds similar to the word *"you,"* which begins with the consonant "y" thus should take the article *"a"* instead of *"an."*

Summary

The indefinite articles "an" and "a" are generally used with singular nouns, with adjectives preceding nouns, and with singular countable nouns. Determining when to use "a" or "an" depends on how the words succeeding these articles are pronounced based on whether the words start with a consonant or noun. The article "an" usually goes before a word starting with a vowel, while the article "a" generally precedes a word beginning with a consonant.

Drill 1:

1. Jimmy is a computer expert at an university.

2. Peter wondered why a information center wasn't set up in the lobby.

3. "Take a aspirin a day," said the doctor, "and eat an apple a day."

4. The book is an historical perspective on a aviator's experience.

5. The pilot asked for an equipment reading.

Correct those articles used incorrectly; write "okay" after those statements that are entirely correct as they stand.

Example:

Wrong: Mary is <u>an</u> sixty-four year-old health nut.

Right: Mary is <u>a</u> sixty-four-year-old health nut.

Drill 2:

1. ___ Indian

2. ___ ukelele

3. ___ wrapping paper

4. ___ UFO siting

5. ___ apple

6. ___ unicorn

Determine if "a" or "an" is needed and write your answer in the blank.

Example:

<u>an</u> exhausted child

Example:

<u>a</u> history test

7. ___ VCR   10. ___ year

8. ___ umbrella   11. ___ ointment

9. — one day sale   12. ___ utility truck

Fill in the blanks with the correct article.

Example

<u>An</u> ounce of prevention is worth <u>a</u> pound of cure.

Drill 3:

1. ___ Englishman led ___ pack on ___ fox hunt.

2. Christmas is ___ holiday that many celebrate as ___ holy day.

3. ___ officer stopped ___ parade because of ___ emergency alert about ___ bomb.

4. ___ great idea is akin to having ___ light bulb going on.

5. Today, Mrs. Johnson will teach ___ history lesson about ___ Ukranian custom.

6. It's ___ once-in-a-lifetime opportunity to purchase ___ ukelele owned by ___ Hawaiian musician.

7. We'll be in Kankakee in ___ hour and ___ half.

8. This day care center is part of ___ unified school district.

9. Even ___ honorable person can make ___ horrible mistake.

10. ___ Eutopean society can never be created by forcing ___ uniform ideology upon everyone.

Comparative Forms

Adjectives and adverbs are modifiers, which are words used to describe other words. For example, "happy" (1st degree) is an adjective while "well" is an adverb. Both adjectives and adverbs have three forms: **positive** (1st degree), **comparative** (2nd degree), **superlative** (3rd degree). These forms show different degrees in amounts or qualities.

Absolute Modifiers cannot have comparative or superlative forms since they are already in their utmost degree. The word "dead" is an example. A person who is dead cannot be more or less "dead" than he or she is.

Adjectives modify or describe nouns and other adjectives. **Adverbs** modify verbs, adjectives and other adverbs, and qualify time, place, degree, and number. Generally, a word is an adverb if it answers <u>how</u>, <u>when</u>, or <u>where</u>.

Mary is **more beautiful** than her sister.
Albert is the **least handsome** of all his brothers.

Do not put comparatives of equal value together, as in "most prettiest" or "more better."

GENERAL RULE:

Use the **positive** form to describe a single item (a "nice" man); use the **comparative** form to contrast two items (he is a "nicer" man); use the **superlative** to compare one item from two or more other ones (he is the "nicest" of all). For most adjectives and adverbs, you need only add "er" to form the comparative, and "est" to form the superlative. Some modifiers, though, require the words "more" or "most," or "less" or "least."

SECTION 1:

Adjectives

Players:

Here is a sampling of some of the most common, and most troublesome, adjectives.

COMMON or REGULAR ADJECTIVES

Positive	Comparative	Superlative
<u>1st degree</u>	<u>2nd degree</u>	<u>3rd degree</u>
sweet	sweeter	sweetest
young	younger	youngest
near	nearer	nearest
large	larger	largest
brave	braver	bravest
deep	deeper	deepest

TROUBLESOME or IRREGULAR ADJECTIVES

Positive	Comparative	Superlative
1st degree	2nd degree	3rd degree
crowded	more or less crowded	most or least crowded
formal	more or less formal	most or least formal
bad	worse	worst
good	better	best
still	more or less still	most or least still
old	older (elder)	oldest (eldest)
feeble	more or less feeble	most or least feeble
much	more	most
clever	more or less clever	most or least clever
ill	worse	worst
horrible	more or less horrible	most or least horrible
little	less	least
dead	dead	dead
lonely	more or less lonely	most or least lonely
less	lesser	least

Rule Application:

Add the suffix "er" or "est" to form comparatives and superlatives (2nd and 3rd degrees) to the positive forms of most adjectives. Change the form of an irregular adjective or use the terms "more/less" or "most/least." Absolute modifiers can only be in the positive form; such words include "only," "perfect," "round," "square," "pointed," "circular," "always," "dead," "very," "unique," and others.

MODEL

Wrong:

1. Marge looked <u>more short</u> than Gabby.

2. Bo is the <u>most young</u> of her three siblings.

3. Barry's circle was <u>rounder</u>.

4. Harry is <u>more fat</u> than his brother Tom.

5. Jacob is <u>gooder</u> than his little brother.

6. Su's card trick is <u>cleverer</u> than Adam's.

7. Justice Yan is the <u>honorablest</u> judge.

Right:

1. Marge looked <u>shorter</u> (comparative/regular) than Gabby.

2. Bo is the <u>youngest</u> (superlative/regular) of her siblings.

3. Barry's circle was <u>round</u> (absolute).

4. Harry is <u>fatter</u> (comparative/regular) than his brother Tom.

5. Jacob is <u>better</u> (comparative/irregular) than his little brother.

6. Barb's card trick is <u>more clever</u> (comparative/irregular) than Adam's.

7. Justice Yan is the <u>most honorable</u> (superlative/irregular).

Model Explanation:

Regular or common adjectives form their comparatives and superlatives (2nd and 3rd degrees) by adding the *"er"* or *"est"* suffix, as in examples 1, 2, 4 in the **right** model above. **Irregular** or **uncommon adjectives** form their comparatives and superlatives by adding the words *more* or *less* or *most* or *least* (6 and 7 of the **right** model), unless they have their own form, as is the case with the words *"good"* and *"ill."* **Absolute adjectives** have only the positive degree, as in example 3 in the **right** model. Words that can't be distinguished by degree should remain in their positive form.

SECTION 2:

Adverbs

Players:

Below are some examples of the various degrees of adverbs

COMMON OR REGULAR ADVERBS

Positive	Comparative	Superlative
1st Degree	2nd Degree	3rd Degree
angrily	more/less angrily	most/least angrily
smoothly	more/less smoothly	most/least smoothly
ghastly	more/less ghastly	most/least ghastly
backward	more/less backward	most/least backward
sincerely	more/less sincerely	most/least sincerely
sly	slier	sliest
sly	slyer	slyest

UNCOMMON OR IRREGULAR ADVERBS

far (distance)	farther	farthest
far (extent)	further	furthest
late	later	latest (last)
well	better	best
little	less	least
some	more	most

Wrong:

1. Ester was the <u>onliest</u> one to sing alto.

2. Ingrid is the <u>most slyest</u>.

3. Dante moved <u>quicklier</u> than Dave.

4. Peterbilt is the <u>most perfect</u> truck.

5. Ruth is the quietest and <u>backwardest</u> of all.

6. Shannon spoke <u>nervouslier</u> than Patrick.

7. Mallory read the <u>mostest</u> in her class.

8. Taylor drove <u>further</u> than Carol.

MODEL

Rule Application:

Common adverbs form their comparisons the same way adjectives do: by adding "er" or "est"; irregular adverbs form their comparisons by using the "more/less" or "most/least" terms. Words ending in "y" may change their form by transforming the "y" to an "i."

Right:

1. Ester was the <u>only</u> (absolute) one to sing alto.

2. Ingrid is the <u>slyest</u> (superlative/regular).

3. Dante moved <u>more quickly</u> (comparative/regular) than Dave.

4. Peterbilt is the <u>perfect</u> (absolute) truck.

5. Ruth is the quietest and <u>most backward</u> (superlative/regular) of all.

6. Shannon spoke <u>more nervously</u> (comparative/regular) than Patrick.

7. Mallory read the <u>most</u> (superlative/irregular) in her class.

8. Taylor drove <u>farther</u> (wrong word; comparative/irregular) than Carol.

Model Explanation:

Regular or common adverbs form their comparatives and superlatives by adding more/less to the original adverb with a few exceptions, like "sly." (Notice that the word "slyest" is also acceptable as "sliest," where the "y" is changed to an "i.")

Irregular or uncommon adverbs usually have their own form when changing to the 2nd and 3rd degrees (see 7 and 8). Examples 1 and 4 are in the absolute form, which means they can't be compared. If something is "perfect," it can't be any more or less perfect; if something is the "only," there can't be others to compare.

Summary

Adverbs and adjectives are modifiers existing in positive form and can be distinguished by degrees (comparative and superlative). The comparative form is the second or middle degree and uses *"er"* or *"more"* or *"less."* The superlative form is the third or highest degree and uses *"est"* or *"most"* or *"least."* Adjectives or adverbs that end in *"y"* change to *"i"* or *"ier"* or *"iest."* Some modifiers are irregular and change their forms completely to create new words, such as:

BADLY   WORSE   WORST

Absolute modifiers are in their highest degree, which means they remain in the positive form since they can't be compared to other degrees.

Drill 1:

In the exercise below, fill in the blanks in the chart according to proper degree.

Example:

BAD   <u>WORSE</u>   WORST

POSITIVE	COMPARATIVE	SUPERLATIVE
1. far (distance)	farther	_____
2. good	_____	best
3. feeble	more/less feeble	_____
4. _____	scarier	scariest
5. little	_____	least
6. funny	_____	_____
7. loudly	_____	most/least loudly
8. _____	square	_____

Drill 2:

Rewrite the adverbs or adjectives according to the directions in the parentheses.

Example:

Mabel was_____ ("excited" comparative) about her new bike than she was about her new doll.

Mabel was <u>more excited</u> about her new bike than she was about her new doll.

1. Mario was _____ ("good" positive) at billiards but Henry was _____ ("good" comparative) than he.

2. Between Marcella and Genevieve, Marcella was the _____ ("lanky" comparative).

3. Craig was the _____ ("handsome" superlative) of the four brothers.

4. Fiona's diamond was _____ ("perfect" positive); Ellen's diamond was _____ ("perfect" comparative).

5. The fashion designer announced, "The _____ ('late' superlative) fall fashions feature _____ ('short' comparative) skirts, and very _____ ('high' positive) heels."

Word Usage 1
HOMONYMS, MALAPROPISMS, and OTHER CONFUSING WORDS

This chapter looks at three sections. Section 1 examines **"homonyms"** (sometimes called "homophones") or words that sound alike but look different and have different spellings and meanings. Because these words sound alike, they're frequently misused.

Section 2 examines **"malapropisms,"** which are words that are mistaken for other words that sound or look similar to the intended word but have different meanings. The word "malapropism" can be separated into "mal" (ill) and "appropism" (meaning appropriate) which infers "bad" or the inappropriate use of certain words. This type of misusage often results in humor.

Section 3 looks at **confusing words** and their construction. Common words that give us trouble when used in sentence structures are discussed here.

SECTION 1:

Homonyms

Homonyms are words that sound alike but have different meanings.

Players:

Below is a chart illustrating some of the more common homonyms.

HOMONYM	MEANING
aero	air
arrow	pointed shaft
allowed	permitted
aloud	spoken
air	oxygen
err	mistake
heir	one who inherits
bald	hairless
balled	curled fist
bawled	wept
base	foundation
bass	lowest musical sound

course	path
coarse	rough texture
earn	merit
urn	vase
ewe	female sheep
you	second person
yew	fir tree
it's	contraction: "it is"
its	possessive pronoun
know	have knowledge
no	negative
leak	seepage
leek	onion
none	zero
nun	holy woman
one	first number
won	finished first in a race or contest
pair	twosome; match
pare	thinning
pear	fruit
stake	peg, bet
steak	cut of meat
their	possessive pronoun
they're	contraction: "they are"
there	that place

MODEL

Wrong: The library <u>aloud</u> talking <u>allowed</u> if students' voices weren't <u>course</u> or <u>greating</u>.

Right: The library <u>allowed</u> talking <u>aloud</u> if students' voices weren't <u>coarse</u> or <u>grating</u>.

Rule Application:

Select the precise and correct word that will properly convey your message. Use a dictionary to determine if you've used the word properly in context, and if it's spelled correctly.

Model Explanation:

The model uses three homonym pairs. One is *allowed* and *aloud*; another is *course* and *coarse,* and the last is *grating* and *greating*. While *"grating"* means harsh or abrasive, *"greating"* is a nonexistent word. The **wrong** statement incorrectly interchanges *"aloud"* with *"allowed."* While the word *"course"* means direction or path, *"coarse"* is similar to *"grating"* in that it refers to harsh. Thus the first sentence in the model doesn't make sense, but as soon as we replace the misused words with the correct ones, the sentence's intended meaning becomes clear.

Rule Application:

Be wise in your selection of words, making sure that each choice powerfully and properly contributes to your intended meaning. Check the spelling of each word and its homonym to ascertain that you've picked the right sound-alike word.

MODEL

Wrong: The governor left her state <u>capital</u> for quiet among the pine and <u>ewe</u> trees, where the wind <u>serged</u>, and where <u>dough</u>, <u>heart</u>, and <u>you</u> frolicked in the cold crisp err.

Right: The governor left her state <u>Capitol</u> for quiet among the pine and <u>yew</u> trees, where the wind <u>surged</u>, and where <u>doe</u>, <u>hart</u>, and <u>ewe</u> frolicked in the cold crisp air.

Model Application:

The word <u>capital</u> in the **wrong** example means *of primary importance,* or the capital city, while *Capitol* signifies a government building and is capitalized, which is the right choice. *Doe, hart,* and *ewe* refer to animals in the wild, but the homonyms *dough, heart,* and *yous* have entirely different meanings and give no logic to the statement; thus they're the wrong choices. *Ewe* should be replaced with the homonym *yew,* an evergreen tree. The word *err* is a homonym for *air* and thus is improperly applied in this context. Wind can *surge* (rush forth) but not *serge* (a type of suit or fabric), so the first homonym is wrong. When the proper homonyms replace the incorrect ones, the sentence sounds coherent and clear.

SECTION 2:

Malapropisms

Malapropisms are accidentally and improperly used sound-alike words that create a humorous meaning.

Players:

The following chart offers examples of how words can become malapropisms when confused with wrong but similarly sounding words.

WRONG WORD	INTENDED WORD
contraption	contraction
slurred	blurred
sales ref	sales rep
virtual also	virtuoso
taxi driver	taxidermist
fleas	fleece
creamed	cremation
bathtized	baptized
preposition	proposition
odiforous	notorious
grizzly	gristly
colon	cologne
comma	coma
conscience	conscious
methodist	methods
germologist	gemologist

chronicle	chronic
floormat	format
autotopsy	autopsy
annul	annual
pennygone	pentagon
part of sin	partisan
deposit	despot
migrate	migrant, migraine
camp pain	campaign
urine	urn
verb	verve
vortex	vertex
indecent	indignant
infection	inflection
measles	missles
carpet dean	carpe diem
endure	endorse

MODEL

Wrong: The speeding <u>taxidermist</u> drove so fast that he just <u>mist</u> a church where an <u>even jealous</u> <u>administer</u> was <u>birthtizing</u> a baby.

Right: The speeding <u>taxi driver</u> drove so fast that he just <u>missed</u> a church where an <u>evangelical</u> <u>minister</u> was <u>baptizing</u> a baby.

Model Explanation:

In the **wrong** statement, the word *taxidermist* is a person who preserves animals. *Mist* is a homonym of *"missed,"* and *even jealous* is a malapropism for *"evangelical minister,"* which is a person who preaches Christian doctrine. *Birthtizing*—a nonexistent word—is mistaken for *"baptizing."* As you can see, some malapropisms can also be neologisms (see Chapter 12), as in *"birthtizing."* Never assume that you have the correct word; always check.

MODEL

Wrong: My friend, who's running for public office, has a <u>chronicle</u> problem with <u>fleece</u> that he says he acquired from visiting a <u>migrate</u> camp while on <u>camp pain</u>, so he wears lots of <u>colon</u>.

Right: My friend, who's running for public office, has a <u>chronic</u> problem with <u>fleas</u> that he says he acquired from visiting a <u>migrant</u> camp while on <u>campaign</u>, so he wears lots of <u>cologne</u>.

Model Explanation:

In the model above, four words are used inappropriately in the **wrong** example. The word *chronicle* means a record of events while *chronic* means long-term, which would be the right word to use. *Fleece* sounds similar to *fleas* (tiny insects), which is the intended meaning here; *fleece* is wool or a

Rule Application:

Consult a dictionary to verify that every word you speak or write is appropriate for the message you intend. Check the spelling of each word, too.

Rule Application:

Some words can sound alike and look alike, so it's important to check each word you use, as improper usage may result in the creation of a malapropism that would prevent your readers from understanding your message.

sheep's coat. <u>Colon</u> is part of the large intestine, which is the wrong word, but *cologne* refers to a perfume or musk fragrance. <u>Camp pain</u> is a malapropism of *campaign* or crusade or organized program. <u>Migrate</u> means to move from one location to another while *migrant* refers to people who move from other places or countries to do manual labor; in this sentence, this would be the word intended. Always check the verbiage you choose to create your message.

SECTION 3:

Confusing Words and Constructions

Sometimes we mean one word but write something else. This section looks at some of the most common confusing words and sentence constructions.

Players:

The chart below offers examples of the most familiar and frequent word misusage.

WORD	MEANING	SIMILAR WORD	MEANING
learn	acquire knowledge	teach	impart knowledge
affect	change, influence	effect	result of something
compose	create, form	comprise	constitute; contain
consensus	general agreement	census	headcount
continual	frequently occurring	continuous	occurring nonstop
eminent	celebrated; distinguished	imminent	impending
irregardless	(not a word)	regardless	nonetheless
expect	anticipate	suppose	presume
liable	responsible for	likely	probable
desert	arid; to abandon	dessert	sweets
precede	come before	proceed	go forward
aggravate	make worse	annoy	irritate
bring	carry to	take	carry away
leave	depart	let	allow, permit
loan	temporary grant	lend	temporary use
suspicion	doubt; mistrust	suspect	distrust
a lot	(always 2 words); many	alot	(non-existent word)
in	inside; within	into	enter
scratch	relieve irritation	itch	irritation
appreciate	approve of; value	understand	comprehend
access	gain entrance	excess	more than needed
amoral	neither moral or immoral	immoral	no moral values
eager	excited, enthusiastic	anxious	worried, uneasy
explicit	clear; distinctly stated	implicit	implied, inferred
intense	strong, concentrated	intensive	directly, firmly fixed
literally	virtually, exact; real	figuratively	metaphorically
prosecute	bring legal action against	persecute	harass, torture
prophesy	(verb) foretell	prophecy	(noun) prediction

reluctant	unwilling	reticent	quiet, restrained
eternal	no beginning or end	forever	without stopping
personnel	employees	personal	private
infer	deduce	imply	indicate, suggest
many	(use with countable nouns)	much	(noncountable nouns)
fewer	(use with countable nouns)	less	(noncountable nouns)
number	(use with countable nouns)	amount	(noncountable nouns)

MODEL

Wrong: My conscious bothered me alot after I sided with Drew during the argument among him and Adam over whether the car's breaks had been working rite; Drew's now liable to think I'm his friend eternally so I'm reticent to speak to him.

Right: My conscience bothered me a lot after I sided with Drew during the argument between Adam and him over whether the car's brakes had been working right; Drew's now likely to think I'm his best friend forever, so I'm reluctant to speak to him.

Rule Application:

Choose the proper and precise words to express yourself; do not confuse sound-alike and look-alike words with each other. Check your word choice with a dictionary. A misused word can give a different meaning to the entire context of your writing.

Model Explanation:

The **wrong** example contains eight different usage errors. The **right** paragraph shows the corrections. The word conscious means to be alert while conscience means morals or values. Among is a preposition used in reference to three or more people while between is for two people, as in the case of Adam and Drew. Breaks and brakes are homonyms that mean two different things: Breaks are lapses or pauses; brakes, in this case, refer to instruments that stop a vehicle's momentum. Rite and right are homonyms as well. Rite means ritual or celebration; right, as used here, means correct or proper. Drew isn't liable (responsible for something) but he is likely (probably) going to think a certain way. The word forever better fits the meaning in this sentence than the imprecisely used word, eternal. And in the context of the above paragraph, reluctant works better and is more accurate than how reticent is used.

Summary

Homonyms (**pore** = close study; **pour** = flow) are words that sound alike but have different meanings. Always check the denotation of these words before using them. Malapropisms are words that look alike and may sound similar to the words intended but have different meanings that usually result in humorous or witty connotations such as "The **ooze** layer has been exposed by pollutants," when the word **ozone** is what is meant. Confusing words are troublesome in writing and speaking. To make sure that you're using the right word in the right context, check a style book.

In this exercise, you are to write at least one matching homonym where there are blanks.

Example:

ewe _____ _____

ewe __yew__ __you__

Drill 1:

1. for   _____ _____

2. tale   _____ _____

3. Mary   _____ _____

4. they're   _____ _____

5. rain   _____ _____

Underline the appropriate homonym in the following sentences.

Example:

Stefanie (died, dyed) her hair black.

Drill 2:

1. The club president wasn't (discrete, discreet) about her actions.

2. The (doc, dock) is where Pat will (more, moor) her boat.

3. Seeing smoke spiraling from the fireplace, Whitney cried, "(It's, Its) the (flew, flu, flue)!

4. The officer (fined, find) the speedster $100.00, which is a lot of (doe, dough, do) to pay.

5. The priest splashed (holey, holy, wholly) water on the (hoard, horde) in the pews.

Underline the words that should be appropriately used in these sentences.

Example:

The law firm (propositioned, prepositioned) the new attorney to work in their office.

Drill 3:

1. The cardiologist (implanted, implicated) a high-tech (spacemaker, pacemaker) in his (patient's, patience) beating heart.

2. The parishioner said, "Our pastor is an (even jealous, evangelical) minister who preaches the (gospel, godspell).

3. The car accident left the teenager in a (comma, coma).

4. Volunteers visit hospitals to cheer children with (terminal, terminator) diseases.

5. The (warrior, worrier) was first in line to pick up the (spear, spare).

Drill 4:

Underline the words that best define the sentences' meaning.

Sample:

(The affects, <u>effects</u>) of the bomb were devastating.

1. "You know," said the manager to a client, "you really (annoy, aggravate) me when you (gospel, gossip) in the (warehouse, wearhouse)."

2. The hurricane disaster forced the governor to (impose, impress) (marital, martial) law.

3. When Rose got poison (ivy, ivory), she (itched, scratched) her arm all day.

4. Markie (loaned, lent) her (hacker, hatchet) to an escaped (conviction, convict).

5. The black clouds in the (havens, heavens) indicated a tsunami was (eminent, imminent) for the (shore, sure) of Japan.

Drill 5:

Write sentences precisely and correctly using the following words. (Answers will vary.)

1. break up   breakup

2. turn around   turnaround

3. cover up   coverup

4. all right   alright

5. may be   maybe

Word Usage 2

Nominalization, "Verbization," Neologisms

This chapter looks at three stylistic forms of word usage. Section 1 discusses **nominalization,** which is creating nouns from verbs and sometimes from adjectives—a common act in the English language. This form isn't always grammatically correct but when the word or words become accepted, they provide a rich addition to our vocabulary. This is how many of our traditional nouns have come into use. Sometimes a sentence works better when the nominalized form is put back into its verb root because it creates active voice.

Section 2 looks at the reverse of nominalization where nouns are made into verbs (referred to as **"verbization"** here, which is a neologism in itself; see below). Many new words have made their way into our daily lexicon by our transforming nouns into verbs, although they aren't always approved by grammarians. Check a dictionary before using nouns that have become verbs to make certain they are acceptable.

The third section deals with **neologisms,** which are new words invented usually by combining two or three existing words to form a mixture or hybrid form, though a neologism can be an entirely new word not based on any traditional expression. The fields of science and high technology commonly create neologisms, which, through time and frequent use, become part of our regular vocabulary. Neologisms may sound strange and silly until they become standard use. The word "motherboard" is an example.

Since the English language is fluid and constantly changing, what may not be acceptable today may become part of our regular vocabulary tomorrow; likewise, what may be approved usage today may pass into oblivion tomorrow. It's always wise to consult a dictionary.

SECTION 1:

Nominalization

Players:

Below are examples of verbs that have been made into nouns. Notice that nominalization is achieved by changing or adding such suffixes as "ment," "tion," "ence," "y," "ism," "ing."

ROOT WORDS	+ SUFFIX	NOMINALIZED WORD
concentrate	tion	concentration
transfer	ence	transference
criticize	ism	criticism
special	ty	specialty
explain	tion	explanation
nominalize	tion	nominalization
discover	y	discovery
draw	ing	drawing
teach	er	teacher
establish	ment	establishment

MODEL 1

Nominalized Form:

I don't have any <u>concentration</u> when Mike and Rose's form of <u>communication</u> rises to screaming levels.

Root Form (Active):

I can't <u>concentrate</u> when Mike and Rose <u>communicate</u> by screaming.

Rule Application:

Write straightforward sentences that get right to the point of your message. The root form is often better to use than the nominalized form since it puts your words into active voice. Decide which is best for what you want to say.

Model Explanation:

In Model 1, the first sentence is in the nominalized form, and though grammatically correct, it isn't as powerful as the second statement that makes the voice active instead of passive. It's usually better to go with the active voice unless you have a specific reason for using passivity. The words *concentration* and *communication* are nominalized (made into nouns) from the root sources of *concentrate* and *communicate*.

MODEL 2

Nominalized Form:

Mark's <u>drawing</u> of a cat was so clear that the teacher didn't need to offer any <u>explanation</u> of what it was.

Root Form (Active):

The teacher didn't need to <u>explain</u> that Mark clearly <u>drew</u> a cat.

Rule Application:

Limiting nominalization in writing and speaking and instead using active voice makes your ideas vivid and precise.

Model Explanation:

The first statement in Model 2 is grammatically correct but it takes more words to state what is said directly in the second statement that doesn't use nominalization, and, hence, retains active voice through powerful verbs. The *ing* added to the root word *draw* formed the nominalized form of *drawing*, while the addition of *tion* to *explain* created the noun version of *explanation*.

SECTION 2:

"Verbization"

The word "verbization" is a coined term, or a neologism, which is explained below. Its use is to show that one can take a noun and change it into a verb, which could be considered the opposite of nominalization. Words that have been made into verbs are not always grammatically acceptable, so you'll want to cross-reference them with a dictionary. Below is a chart illustrating this concept. Notice how easy it is to change nouns to verbs by adding the word "to" to make an infinitive form of the verb. From there, each new verb complies with the various verb tenses (the past tense is used for example purposes here).

NOUN	INFINITIVE	PAST TENSE
impact	to impact	impacted
cartwheel	to cartwheel	cartwheeled
somersault	to somersault	somersaulted
sharecropper	to sharecrop	sharecropped
bank-roll	to bank-roll	bank-rolled
jury	to jury	juried
showcase	to showcase	showcased
soft-shoe	to soft-shoe	soft-shoed
e-mail	to e-mail	e-mailed
ship via truck	to truck	trucked
sent a wire	to wire	wired
blind side	to blind-side	blind-sided
quarterback	to quarterback	quarterbacked
wallpaper	to wallpaper	wallpapered
network	to network	networked
pow wow	to pow wow	pow-wowed
chair (an official)	to chair	chaired
grounded on beach	to ground	beached
facsimile	to facsimilate	faxed
journey	to journey	journeyed
bar mitzvah	to bar mitzvah	bar mitzvahed

Rule Application:

Although some nouns work well as verbs, and perhaps even have been accepted as standard English, it's better not to invent such verbs or use them in semi-formal and formal writing and speech. Refer to a dictionary to determine the validity of verbs that may have been derived from nouns.

MODEL

Weak: Frank told Lindsey he'd <u>ring her up</u> to <u>do lunch</u> after he <u>Christmas-shopped</u> for his mother, and finished <u>e-mailing</u> his brother at college.

Better: Frank told Lindsey he'd <u>call</u> her to <u>have lunch</u> after he went <u>Christmas shopping</u> for his mother, and finished sending an e-mail to his brother in college.

Model Explanation:

In this model, four words have been changed from nouns to verbs or predicate phrases, none of which are considered to be standard English.

Ring up and *do lunch* are slang that have made their way into our daily vocabulary but shouldn't be used for formal writing. *E-mailed* is a coined term derived from electronic mail and is rapidly becoming part of our daily lexicon, while *Christmas-shopped* is a familiar adjective/noun combination that often is used as a verb, though its use is inappropriate.

Rule Application:

Use clear, proper grammar in writing and speaking instead of relying on substandard forms, such as verbs or predicate phrases made from nouns.

MODEL

Weak: After Rhonda wallpapered her family room, she chaired a meeting that discussed how to fund-raise and bank-roll an organization that helps beached whales. Later, she journaled on how the committeed results would impact their goal.

Better: After papering the walls of her family room, Rhonda conducted a meeting that discussed how to raise funds for an organization that helps whales that mistakenly swim onto the beach. Later, she wrote notes on the committee's decisions, and how those decisions would affect her goal.

Model Explanation:

The first statement in the above model features substandard grammar as seen in the underlined nouns used as verbs. Though such words may be easy to decipher and offer a shortcut in expressing oneself, their usage is improper even if they are used in newspapers or heard on the radio or television. Sometimes educated people rely on such incorrect terms. The second statement in the example reads better and presents a more formal and acceptable grammatical style. *Journaled* comes from the noun *journal*, *committeed* is derived from *committee*, *fund-raised* is made into a verb from *raising funds*. Always check a dictionary.

SECTION 3:

Neologisms

Neologisms are made-up words that may or may not have their basis in standard English. Because they aren't part of our acceptable lexicon, such words are taken on face value, but are seldom, if ever, used in formal or semi-formal writing. Sometimes neologisms become standard simply because they explain a concept or label an item that hasn't been in existence before, as in the case of high technology. Other times, neologisms play on words. Be sure to use neologisms only when absolutely necessary, and make certain that you explain them in your writing. Below are examples of neologisms.

NEOLOGISM	TRANSLATION
brunch	breakfast + lunch
chat room	discussion on the Internet
ritzy-glitzy	rich and showy
cybersales	sales on the Internet
catchative	contagious
spongewalk	unsteady movement

brain pain	headache
motel	motor hotel
buffeteria	cafeteria buffet
gymnatorium	gym and auditorium
sneak-peak	preview
mug rug	coaster for mugs
boatel	boat slips

Rule Application:

Although neologisms can serve a valid purpose, it's better to write in standard English than to rely on invented terminology unless the coined word or phrase has become a part of the accepted vocabulary, as is the case with many computer terms. Always make the meanings of such words clear and precise.

MODEL

Neologisms:

The smart card will become politically correct in time, encouraging everyone to be a card carrier because it will contain one's medical and life histories.

Translated:

A card with a computer microchip will hold everyone's medical and life histories on it, and all will be required by the government to carry it.

Model Explanation:

The term *smart card* has been invented to refer to a credit card-sized plastic that will contain computerized memory of one's life history, medical background, or financial information , and will be required by the *government* to be *carried* by the person at all times. Based on the models above, it can be seen that the translated version is much easier to understand than the first statement that uses unexplained neologisms and leaves readers confused and frustrated. Once the neologisms are explained, they become more acceptable. However, only use those coined words that have become admissible in our everyday language, and whose meanings have been made clear in the context of the statement.

Rule Application:

Make certain that newly invented words convey the meaning you want and are easy to understand in context; otherwise, don't use them.

MODEL

Neologisms:

Sharon entered the docoff in a spongewalk with a brain pain and asked the doctor if what she had was catchative.

Translated:

Sharon entered the doctor's office with a light-headed feeling and a headache, and asked if what she had was contagious.

Model Explanation:

Neologisms can contribute a valuable service, as seen in Model 1, but in Model 2 they're confusing and silly and add nothing to the writing. Before using any neologisms, determine whether the words can be easily recognized and readily understood by readers. If so, use them appropriately; if not, avoid them. If uncertain, check a dictionary.

Summary

Nominalization refers to changing verbs into nouns or adjectives. Many standard English words have been formed in this manner. In most cases, this is an acceptable process, though its overuse can result in passive voice and become monotonous.

"Verbization" (nouns-to-verbs) has become more popular with all the new scientific and technical jargon. Always consult a dictionary before assuming that words originally behaving as nouns can be transformed into verbs. When in doubt, don't use a noun as a verb.

Neologisms are invented or coined words that often come into existence from the areas of science and technology, or through the blending or merging of two or more traditional words. Over time, some coined or made-up words take root and eventually become a part of our accepted vocabulary. Other invented terms remain as slang, colloquial, or just plain silly expressions. Check an updated dictionary before relying on nonstandard words to convey your intent.

Remember, too, that the English language—though anchored by rules—is in constant flux as new fields and disciplines develop and yield unfamiliar terminology and expressions. Keep current of these changes.

Drill 1:

1. The child's drawing had orange pumpkins glued on to black paper.

2. Larry said he couldn't go out with his friends because he was on groundation for coming in past his curfew.

3. The scientist made a notation in his notebook about the chemical reaction.

4. The pregnant woman's contractions were less than three minutes apart.

5. By the process of elimination, the student figured out the correct answers on the geography examination.

Underline the nominalized words in the following sentences, and write a "u" for unacceptable above those words not considered standard grammar.

Example:

The alleged criminal demanded legal representation.

Drill 2:

Create ten sentences with nominalization. (Answers will vary.)

Underline the words in these sentences that are neologisms or "verbizations" (nouns made into verbs).

Drill 3:

1. The plastic surgeon liposuctioned fat from the patient's wide hips.

2. Eugene gelled and moussed his hair right after he showered.

3. Native Americans pow-wowed throughout the day.

4. The team scuba-dived into the icy waters off the Atlantic Ocean.

5. The movie director panned the wide scene before him.

6. A Washington, D.C., lobbyist gerrymandered for a new district in his state.

Word Usage 3

Redundancies, Intensifiers, Clichés, Euphemisms, Deadwood

Writing is a skill and an art requiring mastery and creativity in the use of words. It permits us to invent words but isn't forgiving if we misuse, abuse, or overuse them. Thus, this chapter looks at how words are misused (*intensifiers* and *qualifiers*), abused (*euphemisms* and *jargon*), and over-used (*deadwood*, *redundancies*, and *clichés*, as well as how to correct these problems.

Redundancies are extraneous words that add nothing to your writing but extra verbiage. They unnecessarily repeat what you mean.

Intensifiers/Qualifiers are words that attempt to give power to or intensify your meaning, or qualify your expression, but most are so over-used that they no longer carry the impact they should. The word "very" is an intensifier.

Clichés are phrases or expressions that say what we mean in a few words; they, too, are excessively used and, hence, carry little weight in writing.

Euphemisms are expressions that substitute for or replace distasteful or offensive words or phrases. They, too, can be overused or seem coy in meaning. *Vertically challenged* is a euphemism for one who is short.

Deadwood is similar to redundancies in that what is written has no power. Because such words have been used too much, they don't give writing any potency. The word *beautiful* is deadwood because it's become trite and meaningless from extensive use.

GENERAL RULE:

To empower your writing: stream-line your verbiage, reduce the use of nominalization and neologisms, be selective in the use of euphemisms and jargon, and eliminate redundancies and dead-wood. Keep your writing crisp and concise, and always check a dictionary to make sure you're using a word properly. A thesaurus helps give variety and color to your writing, too.

SECTION 1:

Redundancies

Players:

Below is a sampling of repetitious wordage. The left column illustrates the extra and unnecessary words; the right column shows how to stream-line those words.

REDUNDANT PHRASES		PREFERRED WORDAGE
twelve midnight	=	midnight
round rotunda	=	rotunda
advance planning	=	planning
past history	=	history

octagonal in shape	=	octagonal
on a daily basis	=	daily
disappear from view	=	disappear
circle around	=	circle
end result	=	end (or result)
enclosed herewith	=	enclosed
green in color	=	green
reoccur again	=	recur
same identical twins	=	identical
summarize briefly	=	summarize
free gift	=	free (or gift)
perfectly square	=	square
personal opinion	=	opinion
return again	=	return
usual custom	=	custom
repeat again	=	repeat
cooperate together	=	cooperate
consensus of opinion	=	consensus
refer back	=	refer
owned own car	=	owned car
Jewish rabbi	=	rabbi
Catholic nun	=	nun
won a victory	=	won
racial apartheid	=	apartheid
drowned to death	=	drowned
revert back	=	revert

Rule Application:

To avoid repetition in meaning, eliminate words that say the same things or are redundant.

MODEL

Wrong: The author decided to write her autobiography of her life.

Right: The author decided to write her autobiography.

Model Explanation:

In the above **wrong** statement, the redundant phrase is _autobiography of her life_ because the word _"autobiography"_ means a writing of one's life. To correct the problem, delete the redundant phrase _"of her life."_ Always analyze your writing for such repetition.

Rule Application:

Eliminate excessive verbiage by deleting words that mean the same thing.

MODEL

Wrong: The teacher told me to repeat again my presentation in front of the entire class.

Right: The teacher told me to repeat my presentation before the entire class.

Model Explanation:

The phrase _repeat again_ is redundant because _"repeat"_ means _"again."_ Giving a presentation implies standing _before_ a group and speaking, so using _"in front of"_ is redundant. Delete or modify those words that are superfluous to streamline your writing.

SECTION 2:

Intensifiers/Qualifiers

Players:

Here is a sampling of some of the most common intensifiers or qualifiers.

always	too	rather	mighty
very	much	slightly	sure
somewhat	such	so	really
extremely	simply	great	quite
little	terrible	awful	certainly
fabulous	fantastic	absolutely	totally
definitely	severely	a lot	generally
basically	most		

MODEL

> **Wrong:** Brittany thought Beau was a really good dancer for an eighth grader.
>
> **Right:** Brittany thought Beau was a good dancer for an eighth grader.

Rule Application:

Eliminate intensifiers or qualifiers in sentences because they are vague, meaningless, and insincere.

Model Explanation:

Intensifiers or qualifiers add little to your writing because they are overused. The above model demonstrates that nothing has been lost by eliminating the word *really*, and in doing so strengthens and streamlines your writing.

MODEL

> **Wrong:** Luke was somewhat hesitant about trying out for high school football since he had fallen and hurt his knee the day before.
>
> **Right:** Luke was hesitant about trying out for high school football since he had fallen and hurt his knee the day before.

Rule Application:

Eliminate intensifiers to make your verbiage crisp and concise.

Model Explanation:

In the **wrong** example above, the word *somewhat* weakens the sentence since it slows the reading pace, and adds nothing to the sentence's meaning. Always delete words that don't empower your meaning.

SECTION 3:

Clichés

Players:

Here is a chart listing some commonly used clichés with their meanings in the right column.

CLICHÉ	MEANING
needle in a haystack	too tiny to find
pretty as a picture	perfect, gorgeous
better late than never	take your time, but do the task
bats in the belfry	crazy
open-and-shut case	the answer is obvious
rat race	fast paced
six of one, half dozen of another	both are the same
hit the nail on the head	on target; correct
cool, calm and collected	relaxed
crack of dawn	first thing in the morning
trial and error	learn by trying
under the weather	ill
white as a sheet	pale
out of sight, out of mind	if one can't see it, it'll be forgotten
beat around the bush	hesitate, waste time
spur of the moment	spontaneously
bit the dust	died
in a nutshell	to summarize
frosting on the cake	make a good thing better
quick as a mouse	fast
grind to a halt	suddenly stopped
free as a bird	no ties
fit as a fiddle	healthy
happy as a lark	upbeat, elated
as American as apple pie	patriotic
go over like a lead balloon	not a welcome idea

Rule Application:

Substitute more vivid and detailed description for hackneyed clichés.

MODEL

Cliché: Poor Aunt Martha is so sick that she's as light as a feather.

Means: Poor Aunt Martha is so sick that she barely weighs ninety pounds.

Model Explanation:

Clichés are old, stale sayings that no longer carry colorful imagery. The **cliché** example uses the expression *light as a feather* which gives readers no image or picture of Aunt Martha's appearance. It's better to detail how much she weighs than to use a trite expression. An adult weighing only 90 pounds certainly gives a picture of a thin, gaunt woman.

Instead of relying on cliches, write strong descriptive passages through the use of powerful verbs and nouns that will draw pictures or images for your readers.

MODEL

Wrong:	Lightning has struck the old tree and it's now deader than a doornail.
Right:	Lightning has struck the old maple tree and the tree's now dead.
	or
Better:	Lightning has struck the old maple tree, and its leaves have turned yellow and fallen, its branches have dried out, and the bark has crumbled and hollowed.

Model Explanation:

The cliché _dead as a doornail_ in the **wrong** statement is drab, as well as grammatically incorrect since anything that is dead cannot be compared to another. _"Dead"_ is an absolute in the positive form. The **right** statement is grammatically correct but gives little color to the writing, while the **better** sentence creates a picture for readers of a tree that has been killed by lightning, allowing us to see its dying leaves, its drying, crumbled bark that has been hollowed out by the electrical voltage. Thus, eliminate all clichés from expository writing, and write in vivid, colorful imagery.

SECTION 4:

Euphemisms

Players:

This chart gives an idea of what euphemisms consist of, and how they substitute for less "pleasant" expressions and terms.

SAMPLE EUPHEMISMS	TRANSLATION
passed on	died
stretched the truth	lied
civil disturbance	riot
genetically erroneous	having a birth defect
protective reaction strikes	bombings
friendly fire	shot at by allies
societal purging, ethnic cleansing	murder, genocide
liquidated	killed
collateral damage	civilian war casualties
cosmetically deficient	ugly
domestic engineer	housekeeper
under the influence	drunk, drugged
pre-owned	used
comfort station	toilet
economically underprivileged	poor
financially comfortable, well off	rich
hard-edged	tough and mean

between assignments	unemployed
went one-on-one with law enforcement	arrested
bundle of joy	baby
with child	pregnant
follicle negation	bald

Rule Application:

Don't use fancy expressions for direct, straightforward talk.

MODEL

Wrong: Grandma passed on and went to sleep with the angels.

Right: Grandma died and went to heaven.

Model Explanation:

The euphemism *passed on* is a less direct way of saying *"died,"* but the word *"died"* would be better than relying on such useless and stale phrases. *Sleep with the angels* is a roundabout way of saying *"heaven,"* and an unnecessary use of extra words. Write plainly and simply.

SECTION 5:

Deadwood

Players:

This chart demonstrates how extraneous words can deaden writing.

DEADWOOD	STREAMLINED
first and foremost	first (or foremost)
any and all	any (or all)
each and every	each (or every)
appears to suggest	appears
at the present time	now
dull and boring	dull (or boring)
a great many	many
due to the fact that	because
a large number of	many
in the event that	if
during the time that	while
at this point in time	now
at all times	always
by means of	via
in order to	to
despite the fact that	despite
surrounded on all sides	surrounded
particular interest	interest
puzzling in nature	puzzling
in the field of chemistry	chemistry

Other words that have become "dead" over time through excessive and overuse include:

pretty	hardly	always	black
often	frequently	almost	old
handsome	nice	good	tall
thing	happy	fat	long
it	that	which	sick
there	here	many	tired

Notice that many words considered to be "deadwood" are also redundant, and fit the categories of being intensifiers, clichés, and euphemisms.

MODEL

Wrong: In shop class, Linda made a table round in shape in order to meet each and every requirement of the course; the end result was a very sharp-looking piece of furniture.

Right: In shop, Linda made a fine-looking round table to meet course requirements.

Rule Application:

To give power to your writing, streamline sentences by eliminating redundancy and deadwood. Combine some words, delete others.

Model Explanation:

In the above model, the **wrong** example uses too many words to say what the **right** example said in half the amount of verbiage. Notice the deadwood that was eliminated (*round in shape*, *in order to*, *each and every*, *end result*, *very*, *piece of furniture*). The word *"very"* is an unneeded intensifier. Also notice the gender reversal in the above sentence. Often when we think of "shop" class, we envision male students pounding nails, sawing, running machines. But in the above sentence, Linda—feminine—is used to help gap the gender problem in writing.

MODEL

Wrong: Judges of the beauty contest are already in the process of making a determination as to whom will be the winner in the next "Miss Erie" contest.

Right: Beauty contest judges are determining the next "Miss Erie."

Rule Application:

Eliminate and combine excess words to make your writing clear, crisp, and concise.

Model Explanation:

Where appropriate, combining prepositional phrases is one way to cut wordage. The entire phrase, *already in the process of making a determination* can be shortened to one word *"determining"* since that singular word indicates a decision-making process. The phrase as to whom will be the winner in the next *"Miss Erie" contest* can be greatly reduced since the quotes around *"Miss Erie"* indicate the beauty contest the judges are deciding on. Always comb through your writing for phrases that can be cut or shortened.

Rule Application:

Deadwood such as "it," "there," "which," "that" should be eliminated or combined.

Rule Application:

Cut excess words; combine sentences when possible to strengthen writing.

MODEL

Wrong: The principal's office is spacious. It is located at the front of the building.

Right: The principal's spacious office is located at the front of the building.

Model Explanation:

Using the word _spacious_ as an adjective instead of a noun, and combining the two sentences by eliminating _it_, condenses the verbiage to make the writing clear and concise.

MODEL

Wrong: There are many reasons to drink milk. One reason is that it provides many of the needed daily vitamins. Another reason is that it gives us lots of the minerals we need every day.

Right: Milk provides many of the needed daily vitamins and minerals.

Model Explanation:

In the above model, three sentences are combined into one by deleting excess verbiage and connecting others that are similar in message. Notice which words are eliminated, and which are linked for easier reading and more powerful writing. Always simplify, and write in clear, concise words that not only give colorful images but also omit unnecessary big words. Good writing does not call attention to itself through gimmicks. Instead, fine writing should read so smoothly and evenly that readers aren't even aware of the words on the pages.

Summary

Excess verbiage weakens good writing. The fewer words used to create powerful images, the better the writing. Euphemisms, deadwood, redundancies, and clichés dilute imagery and should be avoided. Analyze your writing for these weaknesses and eliminate them by deleting excess words, combining sentences, and substituting one or two words for several others.

When in doubt about the usage of certain words or if you've used excessive verbiage, have experts read your work for their opinion and advice. Also, be sure to consult a dictionary and thesaurus for precise and concise word usage. Cross-reference your ideas in print with any style book, but especially the MLA (Modern Language Association) handbook.

Drill 1:

Streamline the following sentences:

Example:

Leprechauns wear green in color.

Leprechauns wear green.

1. Christmas services are scheduled for twelve midnight.

2. The teacher daily checked the class's homework assignment on a day-to-day basis.

3. Senator Valerie Royer was placed in state in the Capitol's round rotunda.

4. Rabbi Goldstein is a Jewish Orthodox minister.

5. "Let's all cooperate together," said the camp counselor.

Drill 2:

Underline the intensifiers in the following sentences; rewrite every other sentence to eliminate the qualifiers and streamline the verbiage, yet make vivid imagery.

Example:

Cathy always bakes <u>great</u> cookies at Christmastime.

Cathy bakes moist cookies at Christmas.

1. Lee seemed somewhat cool and uncomfortable with the idea.

2. Shirley's too old to exercise really hard for an extremely long time.

3. Paul Bunyan was a mighty big man.

4. Just simply say what you have to say, and then you'll definitely be done with your awfully long persuasive speech on buying a sports car.

5. He's such a terribly poor loser.

Drill 3:

Underline the clichés in the following sentences.

Example:

This world is <u>a rat race</u>.

1. Harriet was so obese but she's now light as a feather and looks white as a sheet.

2. In a nutshell, Einstein's theory of relativity is $E = MC^2$.

3. On the spur of the moment and quick as a mouse, Tara dashed back into the store and purchased the sweater that was on sale.

4. Farmers rise up at the crack of dawn to do chores, and they remain busy as beavers until early in the evening

when they hit the sack to rise and shine when the cock crows the next morning.

5. Sober as a judge, the prosecuting attorney recited the charges against the defendants in the open and shut case.

Eliminate deadwood to streamline these sentences.

Example:

The cats Ebony and Ivory didn't get along; they fought every day.

The cats Ebony and Ivory fought daily.

Drill 4:

1. V-8 juice is good for you, and tastes good, too, and provides lots of vitamins and minerals because it's made with vegetables.

2. There the arch towered, in downtown St. Louis. It's really high, and you have to ride an extremely superfast elevator to get to the top.

3. The well-known women's magazine, *Ladies*, was always late arriving at Angelina's home, so she canceled the rest of the subscription for the rest of the year.

Underline the euphemisms, deadwood, and redundancies.

Example:

My mother's taller in height than my dad who's entering his golden years and is shrinking in size.

Drill 5:

1. A major civil disturbance is occurring at this point in time because of a number of disgruntled protestors at the corner of Taft Street and Wye Street, who are first and foremost wrong about their ideas.

2. Due to the fact that I'm now between assignments, and am financially independent anyway, I'm now free to be with child, and to thus commence playing house.

3. In the event you receive a below midline evaluation, you must cease and desist with all your extracurricular recreational and sports activities after school.

4. Rose won a victory for herself when she was able to afford her own home.

5. Robbie apparently felt self-conscious about being vertically challenged and densely packed.

Word Usage 4
SLANG, JARGON, ARCHAISM, REGIONALISM, PURPLE PROSE

Besides the use of clichés, euphemisms, deadwood and intensifiers, other word misuses exist. These include slang, jargon, archaism, regionalism, and purple prose.

Slang is street talk or colloquialism. Often we converse with friends and family in informal situations in slang. This is not the proper way to write reports, papers or any semiformal or formal text.

Jargon is terminology specific to occupations, hobbies, events, and certain activities. It's usually technical. For example, the computer field has its own set of jargon as seen in such words as motherboards, bytes, modems. In order to dialogue in specialties, you must know the jargon.

Words that become dated, fall to the wayside, and are seldom used today are referred to as **archaism**. It's best not to use such words unless your writing needs to reflect a certain time period. An example is the word "beauteous" which has been replaced with "beautiful."

Using long words, circumlocution, or fancy-sounding descriptions is called **purple prose**, and must be avoided. Always write and talk straight to the point in a streamlined manner without relying on big words or fancy sentences in an attempt to impress readers.

Regionalisms are expressions that reflect how people from certain areas of a town, state, or country talk. Some call this "dialect." This chapter looks at these five misuses of language.

GENERAL RULE:

Be judicious in the use of regionalism, slang and jargon, and archaism; use these only to reflect the reality of a character, time, or place. Avoid all use of purple prose. Recast sentences to eliminate these problems.

SECTION 1:

Slang

Players:

Below is a sampling of slang terms used over several decades.

SLANG		MEANING
boomers	=	ages 40-55
wheels	=	car
hassle	=	problematic
dude (guy)	=	male
let's do lunch	=	eat
we hang	=	out with friends
shades	=	sunglasses

hit the books	=	study
aced	=	passed test with high grade
split	=	leave
awesome	=	outstanding
cool	=	good
neat	=	good
bummer	=	bad
trashed	=	got rid of; tossed; put down
dissed	=	bad-mouthed
hunk	=	gorgeous guy
fox	=	sexy lady
pumping iron	=	lifting weights, working out
yuppie	=	30ish classy
couch potato	=	TV watcher
chill out	=	relax
vegetate	=	not think
wired	=	worked up, edgy
flunked	=	failed
on the rocks	=	drink with ice
rays	=	sun
wimp	=	weak
hot	=	great thing
chips	=	french fries, potato chips
rapping	=	talking
bonding	=	relating closely to someone
jock	=	athlete
bug	=	bother, pester
take a spin	=	take a drive
drop out	=	leave school
fall through the cracks	=	fit no program

Rule Application:

If you're writing from the point of view of a character who speaks in slang, limit its use; if you're writing a semiformal or formal paper, avoid its use.

MODEL

Wrong: Gillian was <u>working out</u> at the "<u>Y</u>" when she <u>eyeballed</u> a <u>hunk</u> <u>pumping iron</u> several feet away from her.

Right: Gillian was <u>exercising</u> at the <u>YMCA</u> when she <u>saw</u> a <u>handsome man</u> <u>lifting weights</u> several feet away.

Model Explanation:

The wrong model offers three examples of the use of slang that would be appropriate if used in a dialog form from Gillian's point of view, quotation marks around what she said: *Gillian said, "I was <u>working out</u> when I <u>eyeballed</u> a <u>hunk pumping iron</u> several feet away from me."* "Working Out" is slang for exercising, while the "Y" is slang and an abbreviation for the YMCA. *"Hunk"* is slang for a great-looking male, while *"pumping iron"* is doing such physical exercises as lifting weights. The writer should not write in slang unless he or she is attempting to make a point about its use, or representing a character who speaks that way.

MODEL

Wrong: Jimmy <u>aced</u> his algebra II exam even though his mother accused him of being a <u>couch potato</u>.

Right: Jimmy <u>passed</u> his algebra II exam with high scores even though his mother accused him of spending too much <u>time watching TV</u>.

Rule Application:

Limit the use of slang or colloquialism to informal writing and speech.

Model Explanation:

The word *aced* means to attain high marks on an exam or some type of test. Its derivative may have come from meaning grade *"A."* *Couch potato* is a more modern term which refers to sitting and watching television, not doing anything constructive such as physical and mental activity. Notice the changes in the **right** examples that better clarify the sentence's meaning through elimination of slang.

SECTION 2:

Jargon

Jargon is similar to slang except its verbiage usually comes from labels used by those on the inside of a specific field or discipline; computer terminology is a good example. Some jargon is considered to be local expression or even slang, but for purposes here, *"jargon"* is used to mean a style of speaking or writing specific to a field of study.

WORD	TRANSLATION
greenhouse effect	warming of environment
sibling rivalry	brothers/sisters at odds
prompter	device for presenting text as cues
spin-off	a new program arising out of an original
sequel	continuing event or plot of an original
readability level	level at which groups read
meal card plan	debit/credit record on card for buying meals
RBI	"runs batted in" in baseball
hackers	computer gurus who decode programs
plagiarism	cheating in written word
subtext	layer of meaning under obvious words
motifs	themes, models
isobars	meteorological weather pattern
script	prescription in medicine
symptomatology	medical terms for set of symptoms
genocide	murdering of a group or type of people
syntax	selection of words and word order
four-wheel drive	specific type of a vehicle's drive traction
HDTV	high density television
codicil	addition to a will and testament
power-of-attorney	right to execute decisions on behalf of another
perpetrators	enactors of a deed or act
junta	faction fighting for a specific cause

jettison	eliminate or eject
software	computer programs
hardware	computer equipment

Rule Application:

Unless you're writing for a group of people who are in the specialty you're discussing, substitute lay language for the technical jargon.

MODEL

Wrong: The professor directed her graduate students to study the <u>subtext's motif</u> and <u>syntax</u>, and develop a <u>thesis</u> of originality on the <u>readability level</u> of 13.1, without relying on <u>plagiarism</u>.

Right: The professor directed her graduate students to study the <u>book's message and writing style</u>, and develop a <u>research paper</u> that <u>beginning college students</u> will understand and that will reflect original work, not ideas <u>stolen</u> from others.

Model Explanation:

The above example demonstrates language specific to one group (jargon), which in this case is people of literature. The **right** statement substitutes "everyday language" for the technical wordage in the **wrong** example for readers who are not specialists in literature. In the **right** example, the word *book's* is substituted for *subtext* (which means the message implied; the words beneath the obvious), *message* replaces *motif*, and *writing style* substitutes for *syntax*. *Research paper* is a nontechnical way to say *thesis*; *beginning college student* replaces *readability level of 13.1* (meaning one year and one semester beyond high school), and *stolen* is a common way of saying *plagiarism*.

Rule Application:

If writing for the general public, replace jargon or technical terms with language more easily understood by those not familiar with the terminology. Reduce technical jargon to simple words for non-specialists.

MODEL

Wrong: The <u>software</u> you are attempting to utilize is <u>incompatible</u> with your now <u>obsolete hardware</u>, and your <u>motherboard</u> has only a single <u>communications port</u> to operate both the <u>external modem and mouse</u>.

Right: The <u>program</u> you are trying to use <u>will not work</u> with your <u>old computer equipment</u>, and since the <u>electronics</u> of your computer has only one <u>receptacle</u>, it won't let you plug in both your <u>phone connector and mouse</u>.

Model Explanation:

The **wrong** statement is filled with technical terms (jargon) that need to be replaced with more understandable words for those unfamiliar with such language.

The word *software* refers to a *program* that will yield desired information; *incompatible* means the inability to match equipment or transfer computer programs from. *Obsolete hardware* means *old computer equipment*, while *motherboard* is the heart or guts of a computer that holds all the vital electronic parts. *A single communications port* is *the receptacle to plug in external equipment*, such as the modem. Translating jargon into plain English may require more words, but in the end, it's easier to understand, allowing readers to get more meaning out of the passage.

Archaism

Players:

Here are a few examples of archaic words.

ARCHAIC WORDS	PREFERRED WORDS
anon	soon
ergo	therefore
lest	for fear that
unction	anointing
shall	will
thy	your
thee	you
thou	you
thine	yours
cometh	come
sanguine	blood red, ruddy
diffident	not assertive
hie	hurry
ye	they
despoil	strip of possession
exult	rejoice
flogged	beaten
nightfall	night
oarsmen	rowers
porticos	porches, doors
wont	accustomed; habit, apt, likely
hearken	heed; listen carefully
whither	what place
avenge	get revenge
whence	where
apt	likely
ere	before
cote	to pass
ague	fever, illness
yore	old time
lea	meadow, pastures
humble	modest
betide	happens to; befall
betoken	show by a sign
betroth	promise in marriage
betwixt	between
bewail	mourn
bemuse	preoccupy
behest	command

beseem	fit; suited for
bestir	put into action
thence	from that time or place
thither	to that end; that result
'twas	was
beauteous	beautiful
whilst	while

Rule Application:

Substitute common (everyday language) for archaic or obsolete words to clarify the meaning of the sentence.

MODEL

Wrong: Whither did thou betroth to him? 'Twas it belike ere nightfall, in the lea of Farmer Brown?

Right: In what place did you agree to marry him? Was it, perhaps, before night, in Farmer Brown's meadow?

Model Explanation:

In the first statement, the word *whither* can be substituted with *what place* or *where*. The pronoun *you* can replace *thou*; and *betroth* can be translated to mean *promise*. *'Twas* is old style for *was*, *belike* represents *perhaps*, *ere* is in place of *before*, and *meadow* can replace *lea*. Unless a character in a narrative naturally speaks in archaism, do not write in this style because it's pretentious, and difficult to understand.

Rule Application:

Write clearly and distinctly, avoiding the use of obsolete words.

MODEL

Wrong: The column and porticos of yore were beauteous with their finely crafted marble that aptly beseemed appropriate for the King and his coterie.

Right: The columns and porches in olden times were beautiful, with finely crafted marble, and likely suited for a King and his trusted companions.

Model Explanation:

By examining the two sentences above, you can see how much easier it is to read and understand the **right** sentence, written in plain language. By substituting "everyday" words for archaic ones that are hard to read and follow, the meaning of the sentence becomes clear.

SECTION 5:

Purple Prose

Purple prose refers to writing that's needless, uses big, pretentious words to make the writer sound self-important and intelligent.

Players:

Following are expressions of overblown writing.

SAMPLE PURPLE PROSE WORDS	TRANSLATIONS
alteration	change
ebullient	enthusiastic

interminable	forever
matriculate	enroll
salubrious	healthful
implacable	not able to please
ignominy	disgrace; infamy
loquacious	talkative
winsome	cheerful, pleasant
demonstrate	to show
elite	superior
esoteric	private
concurred	agreed
transformation	change
ambiguity	vagueness
deduced	reasoned
fortuitous	happened by accident
tortuous	twists and bends
connotative	suggests
demise	end, death

MODEL

Purple Prose:

Having matriculated into the elite preparatory academy, the interminably winsome young man was loquacious, demonstrating an ebullient persona about his scholastic success as a measurement of his future life endeavors.

Translation:

Having enrolled into the selective school, the forever pleasant young man was talkative, showing enthusiasm about his future career.

Simpler:

The young man was thrilled about being accepted into a good college because it promised his future success.

Rule Application:

Avoid purple prose or pretentious language; instead use simple but powerful verbs and nouns to create clear images.

Model Explanation:

In the first sentence of the model, unnecessarily "big" words and long sentences are used to describe what should take only a few lines. The translated and improved version says the same as the first sentence but in shorter and much clearer terms. Readers don't want to have to stumble over long, needlessly wordy sentences. Instead, they want smooth, streamlined, easy-to-read sentences that create dynamic images in their minds.

Rule Application:

Simplify your thoughts by writing easy-to-read and understandable sentences without relying on overblown words.

MODEL

Purple Prose:

The esoteric group of scientists concurred that the ambiguous transformation in the subject was a fortuitous event that resulted in the project's demise; they deduced that the alteration was a result of their research that had taken a tortuous route of an untested and unproven annotative premise.

Translated:

The private group of scientists agreed that a vague change in the subject was an accidental event that ended in the project's death; they reasoned that the change was a result of their unproven research that had taken twists and turns because of an untested premise.

Simpler:

The scientists had botched their project because they had failed to test their ideas first.

Model Explanation:

The model relies on useless big words to make a point, but readers lose interest because they have to wade through too much weighty and stuffy verbiage. The cleaner and crisper a sentence is, the easier it is to read, and the more likely the reader will stay with the writer. Streamline your writing by choosing the exact and best words to express your ideas. For example, use one word that will do the job of three or four words.

SECTION 6:

Regionalism

Players:

Notice how words have been accepted in certain regions, even though incorrect.

EXAMPLES OF DIALECT	MEANING
younse	you
gum bands	rubber bands
boughten	bought
theirselves	themselves
could of	could have
they "be" here	they are here
nowheres	nowhere
"them" houses	those houses
pre't near	(pretty near) near

haven't no	haven't any
git	get
throwed	thrown
awful lot	a lot
far	fire
awesome	impressive
right quick	quickly
straightaway	immediately
frappes	milkshake
good business	practical; makes money
pop	soda pop
fridge	refrigerator
yonder	beyond
threads	clothes
moola	money
get me some	acquire

MODEL

Wrong: "Git them gum bands and use them to hold yer threads 'gether."

Translated: "Get these rubber bands and use them to hold your clothes together."

Rule Application:

Unless a character in a story occasionally speaks in idiomatic (dialect) language or has a diction specific to a region, eliminate all such substandard English.

Model Explanation:

In the model's first example, the word *git* is substandard for *get*. *Gum bands* is a Pittsburgh expression for rubber bands. *Threads* is an old idiom for clothes. Informal and formal English relies on standard language and should be used in nearly all writings. Substandard grammar should be reserved for depiction of a character's personality, and on a limited basis.

MODEL

Wrong: After he had boughten theirselves frappes and pop, he hadn't no moola left so he went right quick to the bank and removed pre't near all of the money in his checking account.

Translated: After he had bought milkshakes and sodas, he had no money, so he immediately went to the bank and withdrew nearly all of his money from his checking account.

Rule Application:

Eliminate unnecessary regionalism and idioms in your writing unless a specific character in your story speaks that way, and even then, keep such substandard language to a minimum.

Model Explanation:

The model offers an example of various dialects that should not be used in standard writing. *Boughten* is a nonexistent word that is intended as an idiomatic expression of the past tense of *bought*. *Theirselves* is poor grammar for *themselves*, a word that is unnecessary in this sentence. *Frappes* is regional to Boston for milkshakes, while *pop* is native to Western Pennsylvania for the more commonly used terms soda pop or soda. *Hadn't no* is improper grammar (a double negative). *Moola* is idiomatic for *money*, and *pre't near* is dialect for *pretty near* (also colloquial) or near. Overuse of such expressions can become monotonous quickly.

Summary:

The use of <u>slang</u>, <u>jargon</u>, <u>archaism</u>, <u>regionalism</u>, and <u>purple prose</u> must be handled masterfully to convey the proper images to readers. Always streamline verbiage and use powerful nouns and verbs. "Less" is always better than "more" in writing.

Underline the slang terms. Rewrite by eliminating or substituting standard and acceptable words.

Example:

Wrong:

Helen said, "<u>Man</u>, that was a hard test!"

Right:

Helen said, "That was a hard test!"

Drill 1:

1. Steve changed his college major because he said, "Things didn't jive when I took up the fine arts."

2. The chopper landed near the accident victim to medvac him to the hospital.

3. Tim's mother told him, "Wash that mutt you found if you're going to try to convince me to let you keep him."

4. Megan refused to let Drew take her to the prom because he was a nerd.

5. The judge was a southpaw.

Underlikne the words that are jargon.

Example:

Some of the programs on <u>prime time</u> aren't <u>P.G.</u> rated.

Drill 2:

1. The Kramers' daughter was killed in Desert Storm by friendly fire.

2. High-tech engineers are calling for Y2K problems by the end of 1999.

3. Living a ritzy-glitzy life can make a person shallow.

4. Mel got online to call up a chat room to ask about a Web site he was interested in.

5. Many people experience angst and malaise in today's postmodern times.

Drill 3:

1. The death of a police officer created a tempest at the precinct.

2. Kyle and Antonia courted a year before they tied matrimonial bonds.

3. Danny was the captain's new underling at the fire station.

4. The orphanage spent days looking for the waif.

5. The decorator said the wallpaperer would be along anon.

Underline the archaic terms, and substitute them with a more appropriate term.

Example:

Archaism:

The obese, gluttonous movie critic ate beyond feeling sated.

Translated:

The fat movie critic ate beyond feeling full.

Drill 4:

1. Carlos ordered a burger with all the fixin's.

2. "It's up to younse," said Peggy to her mother.

3. When Martin Luther King passed, it was a loss to everyone.

4. The watermen on the Eastern Shore of Maryland go clammin' early in the morn.

5. Nate got a job as a soda jerk in the local ice cream parlor.

Underline the terms that reflect regionalism.

Example:

"These sweaters were boughten at Marshall's," said Amy.

Rewrite the following sentences to eliminate purple prose and wordiness; streamline and make the sentences as simple and straightforward as possible.

Example:

Wordy: The most superior mammal has an untoward penchant for terminating and extinguishing the existence of other fauna, as well as that of chlorophyll-producing species through its production of foul-smelling pollutional products.

Simple: Humankind tends to kill animals and plants through pollution.

Drill 5:

1. The yuletide season arrives and announces itself with an unnecessarily high degree of hyperbolic commercialism without regard to its inner significance.

2. On a day saturated with an azure-colored sky where ol' sol brilliantly scintillated and burnished, the adolescent beyond her formative years unequivocally ascertained that this hour presented her a momentous and most opportune circumstance to venture and voyage the neaps and ebbs to attend to and converse with the spinster of the woman who generated and procreated her in the womb.

3. Since the era of yore when domiciles yielded themselves to justly charged edifice supplies, i.e., forest-bearing timber, steel dowels and spikes, paned windows, paneled porticos, and the like, the number of quarters has drastically accelerated, thus multiplying and expanding dwelling developments; however, with the spiraling and indiscriminate rise in the cost of such provisions and furnishings—solely to satiate the needs of the avaricious and parsimonious—these abodes and quarters of all financial outlay (ranging from the least appraised to the mid-line figure to the exorbitant, opulent, majestic, and resplendent chateaus) have now diminished in number.

ANSWER KEYS for DRILLS

CHAPTER I: AGREEMENT—PAGES 14-15

I. Verb/Subject

1. is, is
2. are
3. is
4. is
5. stand

II. Subject/Verb

1. medication
2. members
3. cousin, aunt
4. fork, spoon
5. Chelsea or Allison
6. dog, cat, mice
7. tooth, tooth
8. teams

III. Person, Gender, Number

1. has, her
2. has, are, was
3. are, news, is, medium, excuse, news, gets, does
4. has, workers, himself, ranks
5. was, leave

CHAPTER II: IRREGULAR VERBS—PAGE 21

I. Conjugation

1. burned, burned
2. read, read
3. heard, heard
4. talked, talked
5. caught, caught

II. Infinitives: "I" and "R"

1. wash = R, shrink = I
2. dive = I or R
3. lay = I, read = R, study = R
4. spring = I, lead = I

III. Irregular verbs

be   swing   dig   bind   bend   flee   sink   quit   lose   cast

CHAPTER III: MODIFIERS—PAGE 27

I.Misplaced/dangling modifiers; recasting sentences. (answers may vary)

1. *only* = You will need only one book for the exam.
2. *Getting out of my car* = As I was getting out of my car, I saw the college quad loom before me.
3. *After trying to make a western omelet* = After I tried to make a western omelet, I read a cookbook for directions.
4. *nearly* = nearly a hundred miles
5. *While riding a trolley* = While she was riding a trolley, a friend ran into her.
6. *in my lunch box* = In my lunch box, I have a couple of slices of apple pie that my mom baked.
7. *ultimately* = She knew the letter would come ultimately.
8. *walking along the path* = While walking along the path, we enjoyed the leaves.
9. *Walking over the hill* = Walking over the hill, we saw the valley in all its splendor.
10. *often* = Her brother would come home often.

II. Identifying misplaced/dangling modifiers (Answers may vary.)

1. *After looking at many cars on the dealership lot* = After I looked at many cars on the dealership lot, I'm convinced the window labels have to be compared and discussed. <u>Prepositional phrase</u>
2. *To understand the lab results* = For patients to understand their lab results, doctors have to explain them clearly. <u>Infinitive phrase</u>
3. *Passing the old cathedral* = The beautiful, stained-glassed windows glistened and sparkled with deep rich colors and designs as I passed the old cathedral. <u>Participial phrase</u>

4. *When fierce and powerful* = When tornadoes are fierce and powerful, storm chasers sometimes become just as afraid of storms as lay people do. <u>Elliptical phrase</u>

5. *clearly* = Detailing the contract terms will clearly help to make the terms much easier to comprehend and negotiate. <u>squinting modifier phrase</u>

CHAPTER IV: PREPOSITIONS AND CASE—PAGES 32-33

I. O for Objective case; N for Nominative case

1. O
2. N
3. N
4. O
5. N
6. N
7. N
8. O
9. N
10. O

II. Determining objective/subjective pronouns

1. me, me
2. I
3. her, me
4. I, her
5. she, I, we, them

III. Correcting incorrect pronouns

1. himself, she
2. me
3. I
4. us
5. her
6. her
7. me
8. she
9. whom
10. who

CHAPTER V: POSSESSIVES AND CONTRACTIONS—PAGE 41

I. Identifying possessives and contractions

1. attorney's
2. boxes'
3. addesses'
4. oxen's
5. mother-in-law's
6. his
7. Hayes' house
8. defendant's attorney
9. Mark and Henry's
10. parties'

II. Making into possessives

1. arm's length = arms' length
2. dog's paws = dogs' paws
3. Marcus's artwork = Marcus' artwork
4. man's club = men's club
5. oxen's yolk

III. Creating possessive and contractive forms

1. sheep's
2. it's noon
3. can't or cannot
4. correct
5. monkey's back or monkeys' back
6. that's life
7. correct
8. they're going
9. correct
10. glasses' frames

CHAPTER VI: PLURALS —PAGE 50

I. Pluralizing

1. mice
2. deer
3. buses
4. nuclei
5. pants
6. scissors

7. alumni
8. loaves
9. pharmacies
10. oases

II. Plurals in sentences

1. faculty, are, alumna
2. committees, think, juries
3. towns', sheriffs, attorneys, murders, were, knives
4. products, work, particles, are, upholsteries
5. Our, companies, are, rivers', banks

CHAPTER VII: ACTIVE AND PASSIVE VOICE—PAGES 54–55

I. Writing verbs; indicating if auxiliary

1. became (linking/passive)
2. can do (auxiliary/passive)
3. smelled (linking/passive)
4. skipped (correct as is/active)
5. seem (linking/passive)
6. was (auxilliary/passive)
7. sell (correct as is/active)
8. may need (modal auxilliary/passive)

II. Substituting verbs (answers will vary)

1. drives the car now
2. assemble jigsaw puzzles
3. emitted a fresh and aromatic smell
4. (fine as is; not passive voice)
5. supply information on money management
6. My grandmother danced the jitterbug
7. sell (correct as is/active)
8. Coffee steadies my nerves

III. Labeling sentence parts

1. Louis says Y2K is the term for the computer problem predicted for the year 2000. (active, passive)
   (S V S V DO OP OP)
2. Marta appears mature in her prom picture. (passive)
   (S V PA OP)
3. (You) Give Charissa a smile. (active)
   (S V IO DO)
4. Brynne is the president of her high school senior class. (passive)
   (S V PN OP)
5. She is exhausted. (passive)
   (S V PA)
6. You are relieved of your duty. (passive)
   (S V OP)
7. I relieve you of your duty. (active)
   (S V DO OP)
8. He sent her a present. (active)
   (S V IO DO)
9. The package has been placed in the garage. (passive)
   (S V OP)
10. The child was bitten on the arm by a raccoon. (passive)
    (S V OP OP)
11. Cecily hit a home run during the game. (active)
    (S V DO OP)
12. My friend has remodeled the house near ours. (passive)
    (S V DO OP)
13. The wind blew a large tree into the powerlines. (active)
    (S V DO OP)
14. Every new book has been shelved. (passive)
    (S V)
15. The audience was amused. (passive)
    (S V)

CHAPTER VIII: ARTICLES "A" AND "AN"—PAGES 57–58

I. Determining if "a" or "an" is needed

1. a university
2. an information
3. an aspirin, an apple (okay)
4. a historical, an aviator's
5. (okay)

II. Correcting the "a" and "an" articles

1. an Indian
2. a ukelele
3. a wrapping paper
4. a UFO siting
5. an apple
6. a unicorn
7. a VCR
8. an umbrella
9. a one day sale
10. a year
11. an ointment
12. a utility truck

III. Correcting sentences

1. An Englishman, a pack, a fox
2. a holiday, a holy day
3. An officer, a parade, an emergency alert, a bomb
4. A great idea, a light bulb
5. a history, a Ukranian
6. a once-in-a-lifetime, a ukelele, a Hawaiian
7. an hour, a half
8. a unified
9. an honorable, a horrible
10. A Eutopian, a uniform

CHAPTER IX: COMPARATIVE FORMS—PAGE 63

I. Determining comparative forms

1. farthest
2. better
3. most/least feeble (feeblest)
4. scary
5. less
6. funnier, funniest
7. more/less loudly
8. square, square

II. Rewriting adverbs and adjectives

1. good, better
2. lankier
3. most handsome
4. perfect, also perfect
5. latest, shorter, high

CHAPTER X: WORD USAGE 1—PAGES 70–71

I. Indicating homonyms.

1. fore, four   2. tail   3. merry, marry   4. there, their   5. reign, rein

II. Identifying homonyms

1. discreet   2. dock, moor   3. It's, flue   4. fined, dough   5. holy, horde

III. Using appropriate words

1. implanted, pacemaker, patient's
2. evangelical, Gospel
3. coma
4. terminal
5. warrior, spear

IV. **Choosing best words**

1. annoy, gossip, warehouse
2. impose, martial
3. ivy, scratched
4. lent, hatchet, convict
5. heavens, imminent, shore

V. **Writing sentences** (Answers will vary)

CHAPTER XI: WORD USAGE 2—PAGES 77-78

I. **Identifying nominalized words**

1. drawing
2. groundation (u)
3. notation, reaction
4. contractions
5. elimination, examination

II. **Writing ten sentences with nominalization** (answers will vary)

III. **Indicating neologisms and nouns-to-verbs (verbization)**

1. liposuctioned
2. gelled, moussed
3. pow-wowed
4. scuba-dived
5. panned
6. gerrymandered

CHAPTER XII: WORD USAGE 3—PAGES 87-88

I. **Streamlining sentences**

1. Christmas services are scheduled for midnight.
2. The teacher daily checked homework.
3. Senator Valerie Royer was placed in state in the Capitol's rotunda.
4. Rabbi Goldstein is Orthodox.
5. "Let's cooperate," said the camp counselor.

II. **Underlining intensifiers, and streamlining**

1. *somewhat*; Lee seemed uncomfortable with the idea.
2. *too, really, extremely*; Shirley's old to exercise for a long time.
3. *mighty*; Paul Bunyon was a big man.
4. *simply, definitely, awfully*; Just say what you have to, and you'll be done with your long persuasive speech on buying a sports car.
5. *such, terribly*; He's a poor loser.

II. **Identifying cliches**

1. light as a feather, white as a sheet
2. in a nutshell
3. spur of the moment, quick as a mouse
4. crack of dawn, busy as beavers, hit the sack, rise and shine, when the cock crows
5. Sober as a judge, open-and-shut case

IV. **Eliminating deadwood, and streamlining sentences**

1. V-8, a vegetable juice, not only provides many nutrients, but it tastes good, too.
2. You have to ride a fast elevator to get to the top of St. Louis's towering arch.
3. Angelina canceled the subscription to her persistently late arriving <u>Ladies</u> magazine.

V. **Identifying euphemisms, deadwood and redundancies**

1. civil disturbance; at this point in time; disgruntled protestors; Street, Street; first and foremost
2. Due to the fact; between assignments; financially independent; with child; playing house
3. In the event; below midline evaluation; cease and desist; extracurricular recreational and sports activities
4. victory for herself; own
5. vertically challenged; densely packed

CHAPTER XIII: WORD USAGE 4—PAGES 98–100

I. **Identifying slang; eliminating or substituting acceptable words**
1. jive = work out; took up = majored in
2. chopper = helicopter; medvac = fly
3. mutt = dog
4. nerd = unusual young man
5. a southpaw = left-handed

II. **Identifying jargon**
1. friendly fire
2. high-tech; Y2K
3. ritzy-glitzy
4. online, chat room; Web site
5. angst, malaise, postmodern

III. **Identifying archaic terms and substituting more appropriate ones**
1. tempest = uproar
2. courted = dated; matrimonial = married
3. underling = trainee
4. waif = orphan, stray
5. anon = soon

IV. **Identifying regionalism**
1. burger; fixin's
2. younse
3. passed
4. Clammin'; morn
5. Soda jerk; parlor

V. **Eliminating purple prose; streamlining sentences**
1. Commercials hype and sensationalize Christmas without regard to its true meaning.
2. The bright blue, sunny day offered an opportune time for the young woman to sail the tides and seas to visit her mother's unmarried sister.
3. Compared to years ago when housing construction was affordable and plentiful, today's cost of building has risen because of the greed of dealers of construction supplies, which has resulted in a decrease in the number of homes being built.

CUMULATIVE EXAM

CHAPTER I: AGREEMENT

I. *Circle the correct verb for proper agreement.*

1. The jury (is, are) debating the defendant's case.
2. Either the son or a hired hand (take, takes) care of the house's lawn.
3. My favorite show on television (is, are) "Two Guys, a Girl, and a Pizza Place."
4. Either the newspaper carrier or the construction worker (knock, knocks) on my door daily.

II. *Circle the subject that agrees with the verb.*

1. The (staff, staffs) is donating to the children's fund.
2. The (teacher, teachers), not the students, have been absent all week.
3. (None, All) of you claims responsibility for the car accident.
4. Each of the (girl, girls) is taking one suitcase on the bus.

III. *Make the following sentence parts agree in person, number, gender.*

1. Yesterday, Brett and Terry (go, went) to the bagel shop where (they, he) (ate, eat) heartily.
2. Many homeowners, in addition to the development's builder, (worry, worries) about taxes.
3. Nobody (is, are) up for (their, his/her, its) meeting but members (is, are) ready.
4. Where (is, are) the keys? One key (is, are) over there.

CHAPTER II: IRREGULAR AND REGULAR VERBS

I. *Conjugate the following regular and irregular verbs.*

INFINITIVE/PRESENT TENSE	PAST TENSE	PAST PARTICIPLE TENSE
1. dance	_____	_____
2. say	_____	_____
3. lend	_____	_____

II. *Write the proper verb form of the predicates in parentheses; write an "I" for irregular and an "R" for regular verbs.*

1. Chantal, Virginia, Beau, and Ray violently (argued) _____ with the teacher and (had been suspended) _____ from school; they (had felt) badly _____ for their behavior and (apologized) _____ to the teacher.
2. Troy (lost) _____ his best friend in a car accident after they (had attended) _____ a baseball game.
3. Griffin and Immanuella (drove) _____ through the park where they (found) _____ a lost purse, which they (reported) _____ to the police.
4. The orchestra (began) _____ playing on time but the chorus (ran) _____ late, and thus (kept) _____ the audience waiting.

III. *In the list below, circle the verbs that are irregular.*

eat	destroy	arise	cling	say	lend
forget	bring	bear	sing	allow	spin
dip	focus	travel	grow	develop	sweep
open	program	bet	include	ride	wring
live	display	label	own	shine	stink

CHAPTER III: MISPLACED AND DANGLING MODIFIERS

I. Circle the word or phrases that is/are misplaced or dangle. Recast those sentences.

1. Coach is three times daily offering a muscle-building program involving lifting weights.
2. Looking back in time, the trouble between my mother and me was my fault.
3. Jason will only need to attend two leadership sessions.
4. While singing her aria, her voice cracked loudly.

II. Underline the misplaced or dangling modifiers; rewrite the sentences to read correctly, and determine the type of modifier in error.

1. Raised in Pittsburgh, it's easy to miss the specialty foods offered in all the different ethnic neighborhoods.
2. Driver's Ed students who drive with their instructors often improve their road skills more quickly than those students who are afraid to get behind the wheel.
3. Gradually I agreed to do it.

CHAPTER IV: PREPOSITIONS AND CASE

I. In the blanks below, write N if the information refers to the Nominative case, and O if the sentence discusses the Objective case.

1. Reflexive = ___
2. Whom, whomever = ___
3. Linking verb = ___
4. "Into," "over," "on" = ___
5. Compound personal pronouns = ___

6. Predicate nominative ___
7. "Kim gave it to me" = ___
8. Accusative case = ___
9. Me, us, him, her = ___
10. It is I = ___

II. Circle the correct objective or subjective pronouns.

1. My mother gave (he, him) and (I, me) a lecture on not hurting (yourselves, ourselves).
2. Skiing weather is badly wanted by (we, us) (who, whom) soar the slopes in the snow.
3. The students tried to convince (we, us) teachers to allow (them, they) to go on the field trip with (we, us).
4. Among Bobby, (she, her) and (I, me), we're the ones (who, whom) got the part in the play.
5. The baby looks like both of (we, us); I think (her, she) is cute.

III. Underline the incorrect pronouns below, and replace them with the correct ones.

1. What he thinks matters to I; he could have been talking to others about I.
2. Barb knows he and her whom live in Missouri.
3. Us computer nerds love electronics.
4. It is wise to call I on weekends rather than during the day.
5. The teacher picked on I rather than on she just because he doesn't like me.

CHAPTER V: PLURALS

I. Write the plural in the blank next to the singular word.

1. lady-in-waiting = _____
2. tomato = _____
3. statistics = _____
4. quarter-final = _____
5. die = _____

6. clothing = _____
7. ox = _____
8. buffalo = _____
9. stimulus = _____
10. kimono = _____

II. Give the plural of the words in bold.

1. **Her** _____ **ego** _____ **was** _____ hurt by the **insult** _____.
2. My salad consists of **tomato** _____, **cucumber** _____, **berry** _____, **potato** _____, **crouton** _____, **ham** _____, **lettuce** _____, **cheese** _____, and **fish** _____ — all of which I eat with **knife** _____ and **fork** _____.
3. **Man** _____ and **woman** _____ with **child** _____ boarded the bus, and sat in **his** _____ assigned **seat** _____.

CHAPTER VI: POSSESSIVES AND CONTRACTIONS

I. Write the possessive and contractive form of each of the words below.

1. no one = _____
2. who = _____
3. I = _____
4. she = _____
5. the car of the driver = _____
6. application of grants-in-aid = _____
7. the house of Hayes = _____
8. she would = _____

II. First, make possessive, then pluralize or singularize each word and phrase.

1. blades of scissors = _____ = _____
2. cast of the movie = _____ = _____
3. antlers of two deer = _____ = _____
4. porch of Jones = _____ = _____

III. Correct the errors of possession and contractions in the following sentences. Place a "C" for "Correct" in the blank.

1. Pari's Eiffel tower = _____   2. his' dad = _____
3. syllabuses' details = _____   4. wifes' rings = _____

CHAPTER VII: ACTIVE AND PASSIVE VOICE

I. Underline any verbs (if present) that make the sentence passive. Tell whether the verb you indicated is linking or auxiliary.

1. Burt will be the salutatorian of his freshman class.
2. Please remain seated after the pep rally is over.
3. It appears that everyone has been picked for the football team.
4. Logan's first in his class.

II. Substitute active voice for passive used in the above sentences. (Answers will vary.)

III. Label the parts of the following sentences by using these designations:

DO = direct object ; PN = predicate noun/nominative; PA = predicate adjective; OP= object of a preposition; IO = indirect object; SC = subject complement; S = subject; V = verb, and tell whether the sentence is active or passive.

1. The club's president infuriated her members.
2. Our teacher gave us homework over the weekend.
3. The letter by Kirby is too long.
4. David bought Cathy an expensive new dishwasher.

CHAPTER VIII: ARTICLES "A" AND "AN"

I. Determine if "a" or "an" is needed and write your answer in the blank.

1. __ robe
2. __ orchestra
3. __ early bird
4. __ Irish immigrant
5. __ herb

II. Correct the following sentences for agreement by deciding on the proper article.

1. A honor guard in a English service stood rigid at the castle door.
2. An online browser sent a e-mail to many on an e-mail list.
3. An honest and an kind teacher can brighten anyone's day.

4. A mail carrier brings me an big envelope every day.
5. A ice storm is predicted to sweep through an Himalayan village.
6. John went on an European vacation to London, Paris, and Rome.
7. Bats can hear using a sonar or a echo-sounding system.
8. Mark is a fine young man with an high degree of intelligence.
9. A overly zealous teen sped through our development.
10. A old man stopped me on a street for directions.

CHAPTER IX: COMPARISONS BY DEGREES

I. *Fill in the blanks according to degree.*

1. ill   _____   _____
2. _____   less   least
3. happy   _____   _____
4. _____   _____   most
5. some   _____   most
6. passive   _____   _____
7. stupid   _____   _____
8. simple   _____   _____

II. *Rewrite the adverb or adjective according to the directions in the parentheses.*

1. Gene had _____ ("few" comparative) coins than his friends.
2. Walter and Sue worked _____ ("hard" positive) today and plan on working even _____ ("hard" comparative) tomorrow, and by next week, they hope to work the _____ ("hard" superlative) they've ever worked.
3. Benny wrote _____ ("some" comparative) in the quiet of his home than he wrote in the noisy library.
4. The flu has made Cathy feel _____ ("ill" positive) all day, and she knows she'll feel even _____ ("ill" comparative) tomorrow.
5. Chuckie traveled the _____ ("far" superlative), though Kara drove _____ ("far" positive), too; Jordan came the least _____ ("far" superlative).

CHAPTER X: WORD USAGE 1

I. *Write a matching homonym where there are blanks.*

1. their   _____   _____
2. pair   _____   _____
3. lesson   _____   _____
4. air   _____   _____
5. right   _____   _____

II. *Circle the appropriate homonym in the following sentences.*

1. One of the (lox, locks, lochs) in Scotland features (sale, sail) boats with high (masts, mass, massed), and huge (terns, turns) wading near the (sures, shores).
2. All of Stravos' family members are from (Grease, Greece) where they had (least, leased) some property to (there, their, they're) relatives before leaving the country.
3. The guide (lead, led) the tourists through (haze, hayes), (motes, moats), (desserts, deserts), (lease, lees), and (mews, moos).
4. The Swedish (duel, dual, duo) danced the (night, knight, nite) away on the ballroom floor.
5. The (rode, road) was littered with sheets of (stationary, stationery), showing just how careless and thoughtless (two, too, to) many people are today.

III. *Circle the words that should be used.*

1. My friend has a bad (hart, heart) because she had (chronicle, chronic) (romantic, rheumatic) fever from (strip, strep) throat.

2. Ocean City, Maryland, is a (bear, barrier) island on the (coats, coast) of the Atlantic ocean.

3. I have one cousin who's a Catholic, another who's a (Methods, Methodist), and a third who's an (Episcopalian, Epistle), but I'm a (Mannequin, Mennonite).

4. The poor fellow is believed to have died from alcohol (intoleration, intoxication), so the medical (examiner, exemplar) did an (autopsy, autipsy) on him, and then (creamed, cremated) him, and put his ashes in an (urn, urine).

5. (Optimists, optometrists) say ("carpe diem," "carpet dean"), and I try practicing that daily.

IV. Choose the words that best define the sentences' meaning.

1. The cheerleading (coax, coach) selected girls for the (team, teem) based on their skills, (irregardless, regardless) of their jumping (height, eighth).

2. The (amount, number) of (flowers, flours) in the wallpaper was overwhelming.

3. The (principle, principal) (persisted, pestered) in (scalding, scolding) the two students for fighting; she didn't (let, leave) them get away with their (infraction, infarction).

4. The high school English teacher told her (advanced, advantage) students that they didn't do (good, well) on their (grandma, grammar) test.

5. The sixth grader asked her teacher, "(May, Can) I erase the (bored, board?)"

V. Write sentences precisely and correctly using these words. (Answers will vary.)

1. all ready   already
2. some time   sometime
3. every day   everyday

CHAPTER XI: WORD USAGE 2

I. Circle the nominalized words in the following sentences, and write a "u" for unacceptable above those words not considered standard grammar.

1. The uniqueness of the viral contagiousness made the scientific study interesting.
2. The imprisonment of looters of earthquake victims was an expectation by the police.
3. The judge's handling of the trial was questionable.
4. The best pickings are near the top of the barrel.
5. Research papers require documentation of sources.

II. Create ten sentences with nominalization. (Answers will vary.)

III. Underline the words in these sentences that are neologisms, or have been made into verbs from nouns (verbization).

1. The two men high-fived when first meeting on the street.
2. Nancy call-waited her friend to answer the incoming call.
3. Many celebrities headlined the performance that night.
4. The teacher showcased her students' awards in a glassed-in trophy case.
5. The crowd hip-hopped on the dance floor.
6. Alana turned into a couch potato after being home from school all summer.

CHAPTER XII: WORD USAGE 3

I. Streamline the following sentences.

1. Barry drew a box that was perfectly square in shape.
2. Quinn and Quint are two identical twins who enjoy the same sports.
3. The future to come offers a world of high-tech technology.
4. When you go camping, you'll have to adjust to doing only the basics to exist, and not having all of the modern conveniences of today.
5. Mr. Isaac just became an octogenarian at age eighty.

II. *Underline the intensifiers in the following sentences; rewrite every other sentence to eliminate the qualifiers and streamline the verbiage and yet make vivid imagery.*

1. Miguel absolutely will not write a paper on how to get rid of unimportant words in writing because he says it takes such an incredible amount of time to do so.
2. Julie says she likes to read a lot, especially fantastic romance stories.
3. Al said, "Earl's become extremely heavy in frame since he quit doing exercises."
4. The camp counselor was totally wrong in sending the little children on a wooded hike into what was basically a forest where poison ivy grew.
5. Pamela was really hurt bad. She had to have like lots of stitches, a couple of dozen or so on her leg when she fell really hard on the tree stump.

III. *Circle the clichés in the following sentences.*

1. The shenanigans ground to a halt when the teacher walked into the classroom.
2. The corporate transaction was a done deal after the board of directors had explored every avenue to oppose it.
3. Nathan's idea went over like a lead balloon in spite of his having put his nose to the grindstone in trying to work out every detail.
4. Learning is best achieved through trial and error.
5. Chris was as happy as a lark after passing his physics exam.

IV. *Eliminate deadwood to streamline sentences.*

1. The world-famous singer, Celine Dion, resides in a huge, grand, opulent, multi-room house in a town called Jupiter, Florida, where she lives with her husband and doesn't bother with neighbors.
2. The picture frame was too big for the picture. It made the picture look smaller, crooked, and out of place inside the frame.

V. *Circle the euphemisms, deadwood, and redundancies.*

1. Jake departed in the land of Eire by means of air defiance to study in the field of biology at the ivied halls of a Cambridge, Massachusetts, university.
2. Matt's extenuating body mass contributed to his high cholesterol in spite of the fact that he had attempted to go on a flesh-minimizing program.
3. Cabot asked the food and beverage attendant, "Where's the little boys' room?"

CHAPTER XIII: WORD USAGE 4

I. *Circle the <u>slang</u> terms, and eliminate or substitute a standard and acceptable word.*

1. "Yo! Like cool," whistled the street-smart teen upon riding the subway for the first time.
2. Cassandra was into collecting dolls as a hobby.
3. Liking his new Nike tennis shoes, Ryan said, "Man, these are bad!"
4. Cary said she can't do lunch today because she was feeling funky.
5. Roxane and J.D. hang out after school to shoot hoops.

II. *Circle the words that are <u>jargon</u>.*

1. The hype surrounding the sequel started on television.
2. "Crash cart, stat!" yelled the doctor when he discovered the patient's BP was low and she was shocky.
3. The quarterback was sacked before he could run the gridiron for a TD.
4. The editor wrote "stet" in the margin of the manuscript's first draft.
5. Some people claim they've seen aliens and UFOs.

III. *Circle the <u>archaic</u> terms, and substitute them with a more appropriate term.*

1. "Alas," said the washerwoman, "It's noonday and nary a load of clothes has been washed."
2. Kristin hied to be first in line to get her supply of curds.
3. Church bells harkened that the vicar's porticos were open and service was to commence.
4. In betimes, marauders committed duplicity at nightfall.
5. The cows are apt to graze in the lea all day in nice weather.

IV. *Circle the terms that reflect <u>regionalism</u>.*

1. Dante reckoned he had pre't'near an hour before his friends arrived.
2. Upstate New Yorkers love white hots for summer cook-outs.
3. Dolly from Boston had arranged to visit her Auntie Jean in Pittsburgh.
4. Ally told her family to red up and neaten up the house before company arrived.
5. "No pop or treats," Mrs. Plot told her son.

V. *Rewrite the following sentences to eliminate purple prose and wordiness; streamline and make the sentences as simple and straightforward as possible.*

1. The Commonwealth located above the states of West Virginia and Virginia, and below the state of New York, was, at betimes, accorded the questionable status of steel making occurring in the city of three rivers, but it no longer has that dubious honor; instead, it is now an urban port of white collar and high-tech occupations.
2. The notorious male and female criminal couple—looters and plunderers of the Depression era—were released on their recognizance where they departed the premises of law and order, only to proceed with their previous tour of malfeasance.
3. The students grew weary and impervious to their educated master's constant ravings about his perennial trek through the arachnid and other insect-infested tropical forest along the Amazon, and his other excursions to exotic and unusual places uncommon to the ordinary sojourner.

CUMULATIVE EXAM ANSWER KEY

CHAPTER I: AGREEMENT —PAGE 107

I. *Circle correct verbs.*

1. is
2. takes
3. is
4. knocks

II. *Circle correct subjects.*

1. staff
2. teachers
3. None
4. girls

III. *Make statements agree in person, gender, number.*

1. went, they, ate
2. worry
3. is, his/her, are
4. are, is

CHAPTER II: IRREGULAR AND REGULAR VERBS—PAGE 107

I. *Conjugate.*

1. danced, danced   2. said, said   3. lent, lent

II. *Write the infinitive and "I" and "R."*

1. argue (R), suspend (R), feel (I), apologize (R)
2. lose (I), attend (R)
3. drive (I), find (I), report (R)
4. begin (I), run (I), keep (I)

III. *Circle irregular verbs.*

eat   arise   cling   say   lend   forget   bring   bear   sing   spin   grow
sweep   bet   ride   wring   shine   stink

CHAPTER III: MISPLACED AND DANGLING MODIFIERS—PAGE 108

I. *Indicate misplaced/dangling modifiers; recast sentences. (Answers may vary.)*

1. *three times daily* = Coach is offering a muscle-building program three times daily that involves lifting weights.
2. *Looking back in time* = As I look back in time, I can see that the trouble between my mother and me was my fault.
3. *only* = Jason will need to attend two leadership sessions.
4. *While singing her aria* = While she was singing her aria, her voice cracked loudly.

II. *Underline misplaced/dangling modifiers; rewrite sentences; determine type of modifiers. (Answers may vary.)*

1. *Raised in Pittsburgh* = Since I was raised in Pittsburgh, it's easy for a person like me to miss the specialty foods offered in all the different ethnic neighborhoods. <u>Introductory, adjective clause</u>
2. *often* = Driver's Ed student who often drive <u>Squinting Modifier</u>
3. *gradually* = I agreed to do it gradually. <u>Squinting Modifier</u>

CHAPTER IV: PREPOSITIONS AND CASE—PAGE 108

I. *Write O for objective case; N for nominative case.*

1. O   2. O   3. N   4. O   5. N
6. N   7. O   8. O   9. O   10. N

II. *Circle the correct objective/subjective pronouns.*

1. him, me, ourselves
2. us, who

3. us, them, us

4. her, me, who

5. us, she

III. *Underline the incorrect pronouns; replace with correct ones.*

1. *I* = me; *I* = me

2. *he* = him; *whom* = who

3. *Us* = We

4. *I* = me

5. *I* = me, *she* =her

CHAPTER V: PLURALS —PAGE 108

I. *Write the plurals.*

1. ladies-in-waiting

3. statistics

5. dice

7. oxen

9. stimuli

2. tomatoes

4. quarter-finals

6. clothing

8. buffaloes, buffalos, or buffalo

10. kimonos

II. *Give plurals of words in bold.*

1. Their, egos, were, insults

2. tomatoes, cucumbers, berries, potatoes, croutons, ham, lettuce, cheese, fish (or fishes), knives, forks

3. men, women, children, their, seats

CHAPTER VI: POSSESSIVES AND CONTRACTIONS—PAGE 109

I. *Write the possessive and contractive forms.*

1. no one's

2. whose, who's

3. my (mine; I've, I'd))

4. she's, hers

5. driver's car

6. grants-in-aid's application

7. Hayes' house

8. she'd (she —— her [possessive])

II. *Make into possessive; pluralize or singularize.*

1. scissors' blades = scissors' blades

3. deer's antlers = deer's antlers

2. movie's cast = movies' cast

4. Jones' porch = Jones' porch

III. *Correct errors of possessives and contractions.*

1. Paris'   2. his   3. syllabi's   4. wives' (or wife's)

CHAPTER VII: ACTIVE AND PASSIVE VOICE—PAGE 109

I. *Underline passive verbs and tell whether they're linking or auxiliary.*

1. <u>will be</u> (auxiliary/linking/passive)

2. <u>remain</u> (linking/passive); <u>is</u> (linking/passive)

3. <u>appears</u> (linking); <u>has been</u> picked (auxiliary/passive)

4. <u>is</u> (linking/passive)

II. *Substitute verbs.* (The following are examples; answers will vary.)

1. Burt's grades <u>qualified</u> him for salutatorian.

2. Please do not <u>stand</u> or <u>leave</u> after the pep rally is over.

3. I <u>detect</u> that the football team <u>picked</u> everyone.

4. Logan <u>placed</u> first in his class.

III. *Label sentence parts.*

                   S   P   DO

1. The club's president infuriated her members.

         S   V   IO   DO   OP

2. Our teacher gave us homework over the weekend.

             S   OP   V   PA

3. The letter by Kirby is too long.

        S   V   IO   DO

4. David bought Cathy an expensive new dishwasher.

CHAPTER VIII: ARTICLES "A" AND "AN"—PAGES 109–110

I. *Determine if "a" or "an" is needed.*

  1. a

  2. an

  3. an

  4. an

  5. a herb or an herb (depending on whether the "h" is pronounced)

II. *Correct the "a" and "an" articles.*

  1. *An* honor guard, *an* English

  2. *an* e-mail

  3. *a* kind

  4. *a* big envelope

  5. *An* ice storm, *a* Himalayan

  6. *a* European

  7. *an* echo-sounding

  8. *a* high degree

  9. *An* overly

 10. *An* old man

CHAPTER IX: COMPARATIVE FORMS (DEGREES)—PAGE 110

I. *Comparative Forms: Fill in the blanks.*

  1. worse, worst

  2. little

  3. happier, happiest

  4. many, more

  5. more, most

  6. more/less passive, most/least passive

  7. more/less stupid (stupider), most/least stupid (stupidest)

  8. simpler, simplest

II. *Rewrite adverbs/adjectives.*

  1. fewer

  2. hard, harder, hardest

  3. more

  4. ill, worse

  5. farthest, far, far

CHAPTER X: WORD USAGE 1 —PAGES 110–111

I. *Write matching homonyms.*

  1. there, they're

  2. pare, pear

  3. lessen

  4. heir, err

  5. rite, write

II. Circle homonyms.
1. locks, sail, masts, terns, shores
2. Greece, leased, their
3. led, haze, moats, deserts, lees, mews
4. duo, night
5. road, stationery, too

III. Use appropriate words.
1. heart, chronic, rheumatic, strep
2. barrier, coast
3. Methodist, Episcopalian, Mennonite
4. intoxication, examiner, autopsy, cremated, urn
5. Optimists, "carpe diem"

IV. Choose the best words.
1. coach, team, regardless, height
2. number, flowers
3. principal, persisted, scolding, let, infraction
4. advanced, well, grammar
5. May, board

V. Write sentences. (Answers will vary; examples given below.)
1. Is everyone <u>all ready</u> to go?
   The bill has <u>already</u> been paid.
2. Polly spent <u>some time</u> trying to convince her club to donate money.
   The mayor asked me to meet with her <u>sometime</u>.
3. Roy's political speech became an <u>everyday</u> event.
   <u>Every day</u>, Roy gave a political speech.

CHAPTER XI: WORD USAGE 2—PAGE 111

I. Circle nominalized words.
1. uniqueness, contagiousness (u)
2. imprisonment, expectation
3. handling
4. pickings
5. documentation

II. Write ten sentences with nominalization. *(Answers will vary.)*

III. Indicate neologisms and nouns-to-verbs ("verbization").
1. high-fived
2. call-waited
3. headlined
4. showcased, glassed-in
5. hip-hopped
6. couch potato

CHAPTER XII: WORD USAGE 3—PAGES 111–112

I. Streamline sentences.
1. Barry drew a square box.
2. Quinn and Quint are identical twins who enjoy the same sports.
3. The future offers high technology.
4. When camping, you'll have to adjust to the basics.
5. Mr. Isaac just became an octogenarian.

II. Underline intensifiers, and streamline.

1. *absolutely, such, incredible;* Miguel will not write a paper on how to eliminate unimportant words in writing because he says it takes time.

2. *a lot, especially, fantastic;* Julie says she likes to read romance stories.

3. *extremely, heavy in frame;* Al said, "Earl's become heavy since he quit exercising."

4. *totally, little, basically, wooded;* The camp counselor was wrong in sending the children on a hike into a forest where poison ivy grew.

5. *really, bad, like, lots of, really, hard;* Pamela was hurt badly enough to require several stitches on her leg when she fell on the tree stump.

III. Circle cliches.

1. ground to a halt

2. a done deal, explored every avenue

3. a lead balloon, nose to the grindstone

4. trial and error

5. happy as a lark

IV. Eliminate deadwood, and streamline sentences.

1. Celine Dion and her husband reside in near seclusion in a mansion in Jupiter, Florida.

2. Because the frame was too large, the picture looked smaller and crooked.

V. Circle euphemisms, deadwood, and redundancies.

1. land of Eire; air defiance; in the field of; ivied halls (or Harvard University)

2. extenuating body mass; in spite of the fact; flesh-minimizing program

3. little boys' room

CHAPTER XIII: WORD USAGE 4—PAGES 112–113

I. Circle slang; eliminate or substitute acceptable words.

1. *yo* = hello; *cool* = interesting

2. *into* collecting = collected

3. *man* = wow; *bad* = nice

4. *do* = meet for; *funky* = ill

5. *hang out* = meet; *shoot hoops* = play basketball

II. Circle jargon.

1. hype, sequel

2. crash cart, stat, BP, shocky

3. sacked, gridiron, TD

4. stet

5. aliens, UFOs

III. Circle archaic terms and substitute more appropriate ones.

1. *alas* = well

   washerwoman = laundry helper; housekeeper

   noonday = noon

   nary = not

2. *hied* = hurried

   curds = cheese

3. *harkened* = called

   porticos = doors and porches

   commence = begin

4. *betimes* = earlier

   marauders = thieves

   duplicity = crimes

nightfall = night

5. *apt* = likely

   lea = meadow

IV. *Circle regionalism.*

1. reckoned; pre't'near
2. white hots; cook-outs
3. Auntie
4. red up; neaten up
5. pop

V. *Eliminate purple prose; streamline sentences.*

1. Long ago, Pittsburgh was a steel-manufacturing city that now hosts white collar and high tech jobs.
2. Bank robbers Bonnie and Clyde were released from jail, aware of their crimes, only to return to bank robbery.
3. Students grew disinterested in their professor's constant bragging about his Amazon trip and other journeys that seemed unusual to them.

English Series

The Straight Forward English Series

is designed to measure, teach, review, and master specified English skills: capitalization and punctuation; nouns and pronouns; verbs; adjectives and adverbs; prepositions, conjunctions and interjections; sentences; clauses and phrases, and mechanics.

Each workbook is a simple, straightforward approach to learning English skills. Skills are keyed to major school textbook adoptions.

Pages are reproducible.

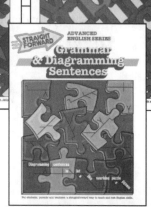

GP-032   Capitalization and Punctuation
GP-033   Nouns and Pronouns
GP-034   Verbs
GP-035   Adjectives and Adverbs
GP-041   Sentences
GP-043   Prepositions, conjunctions,
                & Interjections

Advanced Series

Large editions

GP-055   Clauses & Phrases
GP-056   Mechanics
GP-075   Grammar & Diagramming
                Sentences

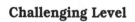

Discovering Literature Series

The Discovering Literature Series

is designed to develop an appreciation for literature and to improve reading skills. Each guide in the series features an award winning novel and explores a wide range of critical reading skills and literature elements.

GP-076   A Teaching Guide to My Side of the Mountain
GP-077   A Teaching Guide to Where the Red Fern Grows
GP-078   A Teaching Guide to Mrs. Frisby & the Rats of NIMH
GP-079   A Teaching Guide to Island of the Blue Dolphins
GP-093   A Teaching Guide to the Outsiders
GP-094   A Teaching Guide to Roll of Thunder

Challenging Level

GP-090   The Hobbit: A Teaching Guide
GP-091   Redwall: A Teaching Guide
GP-092   The Odyssey: A Teaching Guide
GP-097   The Giver: A Teaching Guide
GP-096   Lord of the Flies: A Teaching Guide
GP-074   To Kill A Mockingbird: A Teaching Guide